The Young Brecht

The Young Brecht

Hanns Otto Münsterer

translated and introduced

by Tom Kuhn and Karen J. Leeder

preface by Michael Morley

with further perspectives

by the translators

Libris

First published as *Bert Brecht: Erinnerungen aus den Jahren 1917–22*
by Arche Verlag, Zurich, 1963;
second edition published by Aufbau-Verlag, Berlin/Weimar, 1966

Copyright © Peter Schifferli Verlags AG Die Arche, Zurich

This English translation first published 1992
Copyright © Libris, 1992
Preface copyright © Michael Morley, 1992
Introduction, notes and 'Further Perspectives' copyright © Tom Kuhn and
Karen J. Leeder, 1992

Libris
10 Burghley Road
London NW5 1UE

A catalogue record for this book is available from the British Library

ISBN 1 870352 73 4

Designed and produced by Cinamon and Kitzinger, London
Typeset by Wyvern Typesetting Ltd, Bristol
Printed in Great Britain by Billing & Sons Ltd, Worcester

Contents

List of plates

Preface by Michael Morley

In his 1918 obituary on the poet/performer/dramatist Frank Wedekind, Brecht had declared, with calculated provocation: 'His greatest work was his own personality.' H. O. Münsterer's memoir is above all a portrait, based on the author's diary entries and personal recollections, of those elements which made up the artistic personality of the young Brecht. For (as he notes on p. 46) '. . . (Brecht) was determined that his own life should become his most important work of art, greater than all his literature'.

This portrait of the artist as a young dandy, *poète maudit*, and bourgeois bohemian has lost little of its interest and liveliness in the thirty years since it first appeared. At the time of its first publication, no reliable account of the author's early years was available, the Brecht industry was in its infancy, and the German academic establishment paid relatively little attention to the recollections of a dermatologist from Munich who may have been on hand when the works were being written, but could not therefore be assumed to occupy any reliable, let alone privileged, position when it came to writing about them.

But to a graduate student seeking to find a path through the thicket of Brecht's early work, the book came both as a stimulus and a reliable guide. Münsterer's own personality and attitudes also seemed an indispensable part of the book's appeal and, after some hesitation, I decided to telephone the author during a short stay in Munich in 1968. Showing considerable patience with my attempts to explain over the phone what I wanted to discuss with him, he suggested I call on him 'for an hour' one Sunday morning. The small and rather dark living-room into which I was shown was dominated by two objects: the large high-backed chair ('Brecht would sit in it when he visited me', Münsterer commented with a smile) and an enormous oil-painting of a rather murky biblical scene depicting some large, shadowy and, so it seemed, somewhat clumsily-painted figures.

When he drew the painting to my attention some time later, and, noticing a slight lack of enthusiasm for it on my part, quietly pointed out that it was by Caspar Neher, I had the impression that the 'gaze so pure' Brecht speaks of in his 'Song to Herr Münsterer' (see p. 7) was, for a moment, somewhat keener and more critical. Nevertheless, when I finally left late that afternoon, it was with offprints of some of his scientific and folkloric articles (areas of which I knew nothing and which he had not mentioned once during our meeting), and with the – unsolicited – promise that he would reply as best he could to any queries I might subsequently add.

Münsterer's own personality comes through clearly though quietly in the pages of his memoir. At the time of my meeting and subsequent correspondence with him, he was a man of extreme courtesy and a pawky yet sharp geniality, not easily identifiable with the pen portrait of the young Münsterer as the rather over-correct young decadent *malgré lui* painted by Brecht in his poem. Born in 1900, the son of an officer, Münsterer studied medicine, specializing first in the area of vaccination and the beginnings of immunology, and then from 1945 until his death in 1974 practised as a dermatologist. However, as his own memoir and subsequent career and publications indicate, his interests embraced not only medicine, but literature, painting, the theatre and folk culture, including aspects of folklore and folk medicine, and also homoeopathy; the other book published during his lifetime was devoted to a study of amulet (talismanic) crosses. Until a few months before his death in 1974 he provided thoughtful and detailed replies to my intermittent letters seeking answers to (often naive) questions relating to Brecht's life and works – replies coloured by a wry, sometimes implicit, sometimes explicit, mistrust of academic literary criticism.

In Münsterer's portrait of the young Brecht, two elements are repeatedly emphasized: what he refers to (p. 46) as Brecht's 'tremendous vitality', and his constant readiness to view creative work as an activity that had to be useful – even comparable to an apple or a piece of cake. Songs are for collaboration, singing, and criticizing – scenes and dialogue from plays for delivering and testing before an audience. Those that do not pass the test of the author's and audience's satisfaction are simply put aside, sometimes to be taken up again, sometimes to vanish entirely. Not the least of the merits of Münsterer's account is that he conveys the essence of some of these apparently now lost drafts and fragments and even, as in his account of works like *David, or God's Chosen One* and *Summer Symphony*, enables the reader to share his positive reaction to them. Moreover, scattered through the pages of recollections are tantalizing glimpses of other by-products of Brecht's artistic efforts: the early music criticisms, instances of which Münsterer confirmed he had seen in a letter to the author, and which still remain untraced; the range and style of some of the now forgotten musical settings; and the wonderful description of a special edition of the 'Ballad of the pirates' with accompanying illustrations by Caspar Neher.

The author's tone shifts between the conversational and the formal, often in the space of a few sentences. Speaking of difficulties in the relationship in 1920 at a time when Brecht was intent on achieving literary success, Münsterer observes: 'One day he was so over-polite when we parted company after one of my visits to Schwabing that I could not help but remember the old Brechtian adage: that it is one's enemies whom one must treat with the greatest courtesy. I came to the conclusion that I did not mean anything to him any longer, and I did not want to be a burden to him. A great and profound friendship seemed to have come to an end' (p. 92). If this sounds mannered, it is not simply the result of artifice, but rather of the author's own attempt to convey a sense of how the attitudes of two young men in 1920 were conditioned by different, even remote, sets of manners and codes of behaviour. The Brecht pictured in the photographs from this period is a long way from the over-familiar image of the proletarianized, asphalt-city poet of the late twenties. For all the anarchism and provocation of his stance on literary and social questions, he was also aware that the emphatically avant garde pose was not for him.

When Münsterer describes Brecht as 'quite surprised to find that his [i.e. Brecht's] ideas were much more revolutionary in every other art-form than in his own – where, for all the innovations, he was basically quite conservative' (p. 85), he spells out a crucial paradoxical aspect of the young author's work and personality. Side by side with the extravagant ridiculing of conventions and the efforts to shock, ran a shyness and readiness to observe traditional courtesies which are clearly attested by other accounts from those years – most notably that provided by the great love of his youth, Paula Banholzer, mother of his son Frank. That there was a certain self-consciousness in all this is beyond doubt; at the same time, it would be wrong to see such contradictory attitudes as resulting from a carefully calculated programme. Brecht himself acknowledged the value of the creative tensions that resulted from such 'tacking' (*lavieren*), as he termed it. He notes: 'A man with one theory is lost. He needs several of them, four, lots! . . . You need to know that there are a lot of theories; a tree too has several, but only masters one of them, for a while.' Elsewhere, considering the question within a creative context, Brecht remarks in a diary entry from 1921: 'Meier-Graefe says of Delacroix that here was a warm heart beating in a cold person. And when you come down to it that's a possible recipe for greatness.' Finally, struggling in June 1920 to express the nature of the form/content problem in art, he declares that he keeps coming back to the fact that 'the essence of art is simplicity, grandeur and sensitivity, and that of its form coolness' – a tension entirely consistent with the picture Münsterer presents of Brecht at work on projects ranging from *Baal* to biblical themes.

Though Münsterer is quite clear about the links between, for example, the attitudes (both assumed and intrinsic) of the Brecht circle and their 'artistic' equivalents in *Baal* – 'in those days [1918] Baal's "Chorale" was the song he performed the most often, and it represents the very essence of Brecht's thought at that time' (p. 47) – he is certainly no proponent of reductionist psycho-biography or of an uncritical equating of the man with the work. What he does do is provide an intriguing portrait of the development of a creative personality set against the wider cultural and social background of the times, and highlight at this early stage the collaborative nature of Brecht's creative processes and the way in which his personality acted as a stimulus and focus for others' work. While it is a matter of regret that Georg Pfanzelt – acknowledged by Münsterer and others as the most gifted of the group of friends round Brecht – never left his own memoir or, apparently, examples of his own work, a posthumous selection of Münsterer's ballads, legends and songs was published in 1980* and displays a remarkable similarity of tone and theme with many of Brecht's poems dating from the same period.

Yet these works are not mere Brechtian pastiche or examples of a bland *Epigonentum* or imitation. Both writers clearly drew on the same background reading for their poetic material, and although Münsterer seldom achieved the visionary intensity balanced by a coolly ironic tone that characterizes Brecht's ballads of adventure such as 'Of Cortez's men' or 'Ballad of friendship', the expression of the same anarchic vitality one finds in *Baal* produced some lively results in Münsterer's own poetry. A poem, for example, like his 'Ballad of the Karl May Readers' can be read both as an amusing gloss on literary tastes and as an instance of the author's own distinctive adaptation of supposedly typical 'Brechtian' motifs and images – absinthe, dark woods, vanishing heavens, the torture stake.

> Over the Gobi and through the Wild West
> Headlong they rush with him while the winds swirl
> Made drunk by their steeds as by stiff shots of absinthe
> Through darkening forests no man leaves alive.
> . . .
> They ride and they ride. And the hours speed by.
> The oil runs out and the candle burns down.
> Like spiders in Spring on invisible strands
> They too drift away to an eternal realm.

*Hans Otto Münsterer, *Mancher Mann*, selected and with an afterword by Manfred Brauneck, Frankfurt, 1980.

Editors' and Translators' note and acknowledgements

Presenting the material in this book to an English readership has not always been straightforward. In choosing conventions and finding solutions we have tried to disturb as little as possible the spontaneity of Münsterer's memoir and of the other accounts quoted in 'Further Perspectives'.

Our practice with regard to the many titles of literary works has been pragmatic. For Brecht's works we have taken, where possible, the versions of the titles used in the as yet incomplete English-language edition – with one exception: Brecht's first major collection of poems, the *Hauspostille* (or, previously, *Taschenpostille*) has become known under several different English titles; we have preferred to call it the *Domestic Breviary* (and *Pocket Breviary*). In the case of other authors we have chosen the titles under which the works are published or are most readily recognizable to an English readership. As far as possible we have given titles only in English: in more obscure cases we have also given the German original.

The translation of quotations within the text has been more complex. In his Foreword Münsterer points out that he has not always quoted standard versions of Brecht's texts or of other literary works, but has preserved Brecht's own preferred renderings. Sometimes the deviations are slight, but they lend a characteristic and very personal flavour to the memoir. They also provide important evidence of variants of Brecht's early verse. Münsterer also often quotes fragments of poems, creating new contexts within the flow and argument of his own prose. For these reasons all the verse translations in Münsterer's memoir are our own (with the German original of all substantial quotations from Brecht's poetry, as given by Münsterer, on pp. 176–86). In 'Further Perspectives', where we have quoted from the standard versions of Brecht's poems, we have been able to use existing

English-language translations. Similarly, in the case of Brecht's prose, mainly letters and diaries, we have relied on published translations. Occasional small adjustments to published poetry and prose translations have been necessary, again not least because of the context. Unless otherwise indicated, the translations from other writers in 'Further Perspectives' are our own.

Münsterer's memoir was not always given very careful treatment by his original publishers (Zurich, 1963). A subsequent East German edition (Berlin and Weimar, 1966) did something to clean up the text, but problems remain. It seemed appropriate, for a new edition in another language, simply to correct trivial inconsistencies, misspellings and the like; where Münsterer's slips could be thought at all interesting we have drawn attention to them in the notes.

Münsterer's account of these years with Brecht is rich with reference and allusion. He often refers in passing to a work by an abbreviated title or first line. Unless this signals an important variant we have generally thought it better to restore the full title. Likewise, Münsterer takes for granted that we will recognize abbreviated proper names and surnames; again, we have filled in a little, in order to clarify his more oblique remarks. Anything more far-reaching is explained in the footnotes.

'Further Perspectives' offers a great deal more commentary and detail on specific topics and is intended in part to make sense of passages which might seem opaque to anyone less than familiar with Brecht's early life and the cultural context. We have provided some cross-references in Münsterer's memoir to this part of the book.

We are indebted to colleagues in a wide range of fields for help and advice. The publications we have found most useful are listed in the Bibliography. Apart from publishers and copyright holders (see below) we would like especially to thank Helmut Gier and his staff at the Augsburg Staats- und Stadtbibliothek, the staff of the Manuscript Department of the Bayerische Staatsbibliothek (Munich), Erdmut Wizisla at the Bertolt-Brecht-Archiv (Berlin), Manfred Brauneck, Elsbeth Münsterer, John

Willett, Michael Morley, and our publisher for their professional advice as well as their support and encouragement. Our thanks are also due to the British Academy for financial support.

We are grateful to the following publishers for their kind permission to quote copyright material: Methuen London for quotations from the works of Bertolt Brecht, Insel Verlag (Frankfurt) for quotations from Walter Brecht's *Unser Leben in Augsburg, damals*, S. Fischer Verlag (Frankfurt) for quotations from Hanns Otto Münsterer's *Mancher Mann*, Aufbau-Verlag (Berlin) for quotations from *Brecht in Augsburg* edited by Werner Frisch and K. W. Obermeier, and Goldmann Verlag (Munich) for quotations from Paula Banholzer and others' *So viel wie eine Liebe*.

For permission to use all the pictures, and for kindly providing copies, we are grateful to the Bertolt-Brecht-Erben, and to Insel Verlag for supplying the cover photograph.

Abbreviations

Brecht's writings

Brecht on Theatre: *Brecht on Theatre,* edited and translated by John Willett, New York, 1964

Briefe: *Briefe,* edited by Günter Glaeser, Frankfurt, 1981

Collected Plays: *Collected Plays,* edited by John Willett and Ralph Manheim, translated by various hands, vol. 1, London, 1970

Diaries: *Diaries 1920–1922,* edited by Herta Ramthun, translated and annotated with an introductory essay by John Willett, London, 1975

GW: *Gesammelte Werke,* 20 volumes, edited by Suhrkamp in association with Elisabeth Hauptmann, Frankfurt, 1967

Letters: *Letters,* translated by Ralph Manheim and edited with commentary and notes by John Willett, London, 1990

Poems: *Poems,* edited by John Willett and Ralph Manheim with the cooperation of Erich Fried, translated by various hands, London, 1976

Short Stories: *Short Stories 1921–1946,* edited by John Willett and Ralph Manheim, translated by various hands, London, 1983

Tagebücher: *Tagebücher 1920–1922, Autobiographische Aufzeichnungen 1920–1954,* edited by Herta Ramthun, Frankfurt, 1975

Other works

Brecht As They Knew Him: *Brecht As They Knew Him,* edited by Hubert Witt, translated by John Peet, London, 1975

Brecht in Augsburg: *Brecht in Augsburg,* a documentation by Werner Frisch and K. W. Obermeier, Berlin and Weimar, 1975; reprinted Frankfurt, 1978

Walter Brecht: Walter Brecht, *Unser Leben in Augsburg, damals*,
    Frankfurt, 1984
Arnolt Bronnen: Arnolt Bronnen, *Tage mit Bertolt Brecht:*
    Geschichte einer unvollendeten Freundschaft, Munich, 1960
Rudolf   Frank: Rudolf   Frank,   *Spielzeit   meines   Lebens*,
    Heidelberg, 1960
Artur Kutscher: Artur Kutscher, *Der Theaterprofessor: ein*
    Leben für die Wissenschaft vom Theater, Munich, 1960
Mancher Mann: Hanns Otto Münsterer, *Mancher Mann*, selec-
    ted writings, edited with an Afterword by Manfred
    Brauneck, Frankfurt, 1980
So viel wie eine Liebe: Paula Banholzer and others, *So viel wie*
    eine Liebe: Der unbekannte Brecht, edited by Axel Polder and
    Willibald Eser, Munich, 1981

Editorial Introduction

Bertolt Brecht's early years and development as a writer cannot easily be reconciled with what we know of the older political poet and playwright. Their chaotic and exuberant variousness does not make for neat literary biography. Moreover, much Brecht criticism has been motivated, or at least shadowed, by more modern political divisions. Commentators have often swept lightly over Brecht's origins. They have been inclined to associate his name above all with the Berlin of the progressive Weimar Republic or of the founding years of the socialist state of the German Democratic Republic, or else with the wandering anti-fascist exile of the years between. However, the young Brecht, Eugen Berthold Friedrich, was born and raised in Augsburg. It was here in the heart of Bavarian Swabia that he spent most of the first twenty-four years of his life and grew to become the familiar 'Bert Brecht'. The importance of these years for his writing should not be underestimated. The recent disintegration of Cold War rivalries offers an opportunity to reassess this young Brecht, and to find our way back to a life before the decades of political, cultural and critical obfuscation.

Hanns Otto Münsterer's recollections of his youthful friendship with Brecht are the most important and most complete first-hand account we have of Brecht's literary coming-of-age. They have long formed an essential source for our knowledge and understanding of Brecht as a young writer. In compiling his account, in the early nineteen sixties, Münsterer appears to have been motivated primarily by a desire to serve the cause of scholarship and by the conviction that the time had come to communicate valuable facts and insights. In the Foreword he explains how he hopes that his memories of texts and of circumstances will lead to the rediscovery of works believed lost, and to a clear chronology of Brecht's early work. He can scarcely have anticipated just how many of the pieces he mentions would indeed turn up within the next decades – although quite a number remain untraced (see the Bibliography for German and English publications). However, Münsterer also offers insights into a whole host of other important matters, such as Brecht's early reading habits, interests and influences, his attitudes and his methods of composition. In the years since the work's first publication, much more has come to light to corroborate – or occasionally to correct – his version of events.

Münsterer was born in 1900, two years Brecht's junior, in Dieuze in Lorraine (then German). His family settled in Augsburg before the First World War. It is perhaps above all the congruence of the geographical, historical and cultural perspectives of their youths which makes Münsterer's memoir of Brecht so valuable. In the years covered by this book they shared many sympathies and ambitions. In later life they drifted far apart. In striking contrast to Brecht, Münsterer only ever moved as far as Munich; he remained in Bavaria throughout the twenties, throughout the years of Nazi rule and the war, right up to his death in 1974. In 1933 he married an Augsburg girl, Elsbeth Nebelung. In 1937 Münsterer, whose political sympathies speak clearly through the pages of his memoir, was expelled from the National Socialist Chamber of Literature and forbidden to write. In the forties, however, he made a considerable name for himself as a doctor of medicine, specializing in dermatology and virology; in later life he devoted himself increasingly to the study of popular medicine and religious art (see Bibliography).

One might expect Münsterer's memories to be dulled in places, embellished in others. However, his Brecht book is an unusual document: it was written for the most part only after detailed reference to his own diary from the same period. At several points in the text he refers explicitly to his diary notebooks, presumably lying open on the desk next to him as he undertook his reconstruction. Since a few scraps of those notebooks have now been released for publication, we can observe the process of composition by comparing parallel passages (see e.g.

pp. 57–9 and 144–6). Apart from his diaries, Münsterer took careful notice of documentary sources and other published accounts, to which he also makes explicit reference. In most points of fact, in so far as these can be checked, he appears to be reliable. The very precision of his memories of conversations and of versions of Brecht's texts may at first reading seem implausible. However we know from the diary that he kept quite a full record of the things which seemed of value to him then (like the remark about Bolshevism on p. 146). Moreover, in many cases Münsterer owned an early typescript transcription or a newspaper cutting of the poem he quotes. Amongst the files of Brechtiana preserved with his papers in the Bavarian State Library there is a lovingly bound volume of typescripts with tantalizing notes like: 'From the manuscript', or 'Orally 1922', or 'Orally, but definitely word-perfect'.

On the other hand, there are limitations to Münsterer's portrait of the young Brecht. There are some things he simply did not know very much about; he was not always one of the inner circle and there is no reason to suppose that Brecht shared his most intimate personal experiences with him. For example, it seems likely that Münsterer was not much aware of Brecht's concern with his physical frailty and his heart problems – which loom large in Paula Banholzer's account. There are clearly also matters which he deliberately suppressed. He opens one chapter with the remark that 'reminiscences of Brecht's . . . upbringing will be of little interest to literary historians' (p. 39). Often we might prefer to have done without that self-censoring filter. Amongst the matters he passes by more out of a sense of tact is the story of Brecht's interest in Therese Ostheimer. To this, as to other salacious anecdotes, he alludes only obliquely (pp. 69–70). There are two particularly important issues which Münsterer discreetly hushes up. The first is the full extent of Brecht's involvement with Paula Banholzer and the significance for Brecht of the birth of his son. Here again, he may not have known quite what was going on, at least until it was all over. The second concerns Münsterer's own family's financial problems, and the extent of his personal crisis in 1919. It has only been with the help of his

widow, Elsbeth Münsterer, that we have been able to make sense
of some of his more opaque hints.* Finally, Münsterer's whole
interpretation of events is of course coloured – by the admiration
he felt in his youth for the older poet, and by the later mature
respect, as well as by the intervening years between those original
notes and the decision to publish, some forty years on.

In the writing up, Münsterer made little attempt to smooth
over the traces of the passing years; we are made continually
aware of the process of sifting through old documents, and how
that in turn provokes further memories and new thoughts. Münsterer's text is full of shifts in register: from the passionate
involvement of the young man to the benevolent irony of the
older. The style never settles down; it mixes cultured reflections
with deflations, nostalgia for lost youth, vulgarities and sudden
bursts of colloquialism. In its content too the text betrays the dual
perspective of the cultivated German: it makes frequent allusion
to the situation in the aftermath of the First World War, and then
also to the years of recovery after the Second. Münsterer has an
easy familiarity, not just with the details of Brecht's early life, but
also with the changing set of cultural coordinates which defined
the horizons of a particular generation.

It is particularly interesting to compare Münsterer's account
with some of the other sources concerned with the young Brecht,
extracts from which we have collected in 'Further Perspectives'.
Amongst the first-hand biographical sketches, few remain
uncoloured by prejudice, and some – despite their otherwise
serious intent – are marred by the effort to reap a little reflected
glory or to make much of just a few anecdotes. The earlier pieces
in Hubert Witt's book (see the Bibliography for this and for all
sources quoted), originally compiled around the same time as
Münsterer's memoir, often suffers from such flaws. There are
literary critical sketches too, which attempt to arrive at an assess-
ment of some aspect of a writer who was already being compared
to Goethe. In Arnolt Bronnen's memoir (see e.g. pp. 119 and
169–71), written in the fifties, we have something rather different

*We are indebted to Manfred Brauneck for passing on Frau Münsterer's
explanations of a number of obscure passages.

– a highly stylized literary autobiography, which is as much an attempt by Bronnen to rehabilitate himself after his involvement in the Third Reich, as it is a study of Brecht. It is not so openly a fiction as Feuchtwanger's literary portraits or Brecht's own *Refugee Conversations*; none the less, like these it needs to be used with caution and alongside other accounts.

The early nineteen eighties saw the publication of two books on which we have drawn extensively in 'Further Perspectives', and which require particular explanation. Walter Brecht's memories of his older brother are told from the perspective of the family; he offers few insights into Brecht's social and literary lives outside the Bleichstraße. Walter Brecht writes with quite deliberate hindsight; his book has less immediacy than Münsterer's and is coloured by a brotherly resentment at Eugen Berthold's airs, highhandedness and, ultimately, greatness. None the less, the family angle is important, and the book yields valuable insights. A further interesting comparison is provided by the volume *So viel wie eine Liebe*. This is a compendium of the experiences of some of the women in the young Brecht's life, particularly Paula Banholzer who bore his first child. It is divided into sections: Paula Banholzer's own account of her relationship with Brecht (pp. 7–99), an interview with Banholzer conducted by the editors of the book (pp. 103–49), a further interview with Marianne Zoff, Brecht's first wife (pp. 151–93) and, finally, impressionistic reports and accounts of conversations with a range of other acquaintances. Paula Banholzer had evidently collected her memories, partly in her head and partly on paper, for some time before eventual publication. She is, however, even more determined than Walter Brecht that she has no literary pretensions; and she has none of the cultural education of Münsterer. However, its very straightforwardness gives her story spontaneity and liveliness.

Clearly, all of these documents, like those fragments of interviews, conversations and correspondences collected in the volume *Brecht in Augsburg*, need to be approached carefully, and all rather differently. They have often been used somewhat uncritically by biographers. We have sought to illuminate them mutually by juxtaposition and comparison. The extracts presented in 'Further Perspectives', many from sources which have only come to light since Münsterer's death, do not therefore serve only to relativize Münsterer's own story, they also add to its value. Münsterer himself was after all well aware that his portrait of Brecht could be only a partial one.

There is, however, a further source invaluable to an understanding of the young Brecht; that is Brecht's own voice. Many of the large number of his letters surviving from this period, as well as the diaries from 1920–22, are now available in English. They furnish a fascinating range of essential 'further perspectives'. Of course, they are still not to be read at face value. On the contrary, they present a bewildering multiplicity of self-stylizations. They offer insights into the workings of the poet and the ways of the man, at his dangerously attractive best and at his chauvinistic worst. There are, moreover, documents from Brecht's youth still to be published; Brecht's letters to Marianne Zoff, for example, have only very recently appeared.

The friendship between Brecht and Münsterer provides us not only with a valuable guide to the young writer, but also with a tantalizing portrait of a literary friendship. What was the nature of this relationship? Here again Münsterer has been somewhat unforthcoming. The friendship was brief, lasting really only a couple of years. For Münsterer, however, it was very intense. Brecht was the older of the two, a self-possessed young man, a 'real poet', an apparently petty-bourgeois rebel from the workers' suburbs. Münsterer was still very much a schoolboy, the son of a cavalry major, whose family had fallen on hard times but still lived in some splendour on one of the main streets of Augsburg. For a short while they saw each other nearly every day. Even much later Münsterer writes with scarcely concealed emotion of their times together, swimming in the Lech and lazing in the grass, or walking under the stars through Augsburg. Yet, from Brecht's perspective it may have been rather different. There are very few letters from Brecht to Münsterer, unlike to Caspar Neher or Paula Banholzer for example, and much of the time the younger man is addressed formally as 'Herr Münsterer'. In contrast to Neher, Münsterer was never at the Front and perhaps never far enough away to merit a proper correspondence; and the formal address was certainly to some extent a stylization of the elegantly besuited young man who came to visit Brecht in the autumn of 1917. Nevertheless, there is little passion in the letters we do have, and apart from 'Song to Herr Münsterer' (p. 7) there are no other works dedicated or devoted to the young disciple. The friendships with Cas (Neher) and Orge (Pfanzelt) surely meant more to Brecht.

In fact Münsterer was one of a whole band of gifted friends, inspiring each other and driving each other on to ever more extravagant but also greater artistic endeavours. As he relates, many of them were engaged in writing, and on occasion Brecht would take up one of the others' compositions and refashion it as his own poem (see p. 86). One of the most valuable features of Münsterer's memoir is the vivid characterization of this sort of production team, as well as of the fascinating man at its centre. Later, Brecht and his critics would theorize this as the collectivization of the artistic process. It seems plain that it was not Brecht alone who profited from such joint efforts. Indeed there are strong suggestions that the traffic of inspiration and creation was two-way. Münsterer contends that the association with Brecht enriched everyone's lives.

Nevertheless, before long the line between collaboration and exploitation became blurred. In his description of the rehearsals for *Drums in the Night*, Münsterer suggests that he himself came to perform a function analogous to that of Brecht's later collaborative theatre teams (p. 103). In fact his own role, although certainly not passive, was increasingly a secondary and supportive one: as the go-between in relationships with women, interceding with publishers, writing reviews, and so on. In his unselfish promotion of Brecht's career and interests, Münsterer seems sometimes to prefigure those later loyal followers (many of them women, such as Elisabeth Hauptmann) who effaced themselves in order to serve what they recognized as genius. On the one hand, Münsterer's account inevitably seeks to underline the importance of his and Brecht's friendship. In his final chapter he compares them with the illustrious couples, Lotte and Goethe, Verlaine and Rimbaud. On the other hand, there is the humble, almost pathetic self-abasement of his final sentences. His relationship with Brecht was, it seems, a large part of Münsterer's life; it was apparently only a small part of Brecht's.

And yet we clearly need to address Münsterer as a poet and writer in his own right too. Some of his work might perhaps best be described as derivative. But that is not the end of it. The fact that he wrote poems on some of the same themes as Brecht – the swingboats, or the exploits of early aviators (see pp. 128 and 43) – is evidence also of that mixture of cultural influences and individual talents out of which both men emerged. Münsterer's own early literary efforts at least run parallel, and ultimately issue into his own quite distinctive achievement. To mention just one interesting example, amongst Münsterer's unpublished papers there is a sheet of his own headed notepaper dated 1938 with an ironic anti-Nazi protest song in the form of a popular chorale, with striking similarities to Brecht's own parodistic 'Hitler-Chorales'. Yet, cut off as they were from one another, Münsterer would hardly have known that Brecht had experimented with the very same form in exile. This is not imitation, but an independent development from the same roots. Besides, Münsterer did not only write poems with Brecht, under Brecht's influence; indeed his real growth as a writer started afterwards. Throughout the twenties and thirties, and right up to the nineteen sixties, Münsterer continued to write, and despite his reluctance to publish or become involved in a literary scene, a number of his poems appeared in leading literary journals or were broadcast on the radio (see Bibliography).

The friendship between Brecht and Münsterer flourished above all – his memoir shows this – when they read, talked about, wrote, or otherwise shared their experiences of literature. Nevertheless, Münsterer seems sometimes unaware of the extent to which the young Brecht and he himself were fictionalizing elements of their own lived experience, in order to make literature out of it. Paula Banholzer remarks on the proximity of truth and fiction for Brecht. To take a concrete example: she tells how he

felt sick and scared on the swing-boats (see p. 127); for Brecht
and for Münsterer, on the other hand, the swing-boats were an
ecstatic metaphor, and the stuff of poems (see pp. 68–9 and 127–
8). To some degree this indicates the different temperaments of
the two memoir writers; but it also helps to characterize the
sphere in which Brecht and Münsterer could be friends. At their
first meeting they exchanged poems; and it seems that their
friendship remained very much in the realm of literature. When,
for example, we find parts of Baal's dialogue with Johannes about
women and love (Scene 2 of *Baal*) in Münsterer's diary –
apparently recorded as an actual conversation – it becomes difficult to say quite where the fiction set in. Certainly, when Münsterer tells us of the friends' flirtation with the ethos of Baal
(p. 63), we should not therefore suppose that Brecht ever behaved
at all like his anarchic and debauched character. On the contrary,
as Banholzer reveals and as Münsterer himself also assures us,
Brecht was in many ways a very shy and cautious young man,
obsessed with control and self-control. Although in his literature
he was exploiting experience, it was experience as much dreamt of
as lived. Just as much as the whole gang of friends shared a real
life, so they shared also a life of the imagination.

The years covered by Münsterer's narrative, in Augsburg and
Munich, were for Brecht the years in which he learnt to control
and to make use of all these creative processes and of these friendships. It started as a period of quite exceptional and chaotic
productivity; in this respect the year 1919 was perhaps the high
point. Münsterer describes the stream of works issuing
from Brecht's blend of spontaneity and reflection, of instinct
and reason. The memoir is a source of countless insights into
the origins and processes of Brecht's early compositions. But
Münsterer also describes what retrospective biographies of the
successful writer so easily overlook: the effort and the disappointments. He describes the greater method and purpose which were
required in order to enter literature as a profession; in this respect
1922 was the breakthrough. And so we have an image of the years
in which Brecht 'made it', and we have an image of the worlds
and the fictions out of which he made it.

In Münsterer's account Brecht sometimes seems a bundle of wild eclecticisms and bewildering inconsistencies – in his literary practice and ideas, in his beliefs, philosophies, aesthetics, and in his social behaviour. Those who are seeking to explain his later political commitment argue that, as a young man, he was just looking for something to believe in. But that is not a necessary conclusion. The sort of experimental montage which Brecht developed in fact reveals a clear kinship with the work of Wedekind, whom he so much admired. The eclecticisms and juxtapositions are simply becoming a self-conscious method. Reading this first-hand account, it appears less acceptable than ever to seek to harmonize the young poet's many parts into a coherent development towards the familiar politicized literary persona.

This English edition of Hanns Otto Münsterer's memories and conversations with Brecht is intended to illuminate, for the general reader and the specialist alike, the early life of one of the twentieth century's most important and controversial writers. Perhaps it will also stimulate renewed scholarly interest in Münsterer's not inconsiderable achievement.

Tom Kuhn
Karen J. Leeder
December 1991

The Young Brecht

Ja, damals waren wir Dichter.

Of course, we were poets then.   Hanns Otto Münsterer

I first saw the light of the world in 1898. My parents hail from the Black Forest. Elementary school bored me for four years. In the nine years of my pickling at the Augsburg Realgymnasium I made no great contribution to my teachers' advancement. They never tired of pointing out my penchant for idleness and independence. At the university I read medicine and learned to play the guitar. At secondary school I had gone in for all kinds of sport and developed a heart condition, which familiarized me with the secrets of metaphysics. During the revolution, I served as an orderly in a military hospital. After that I wrote a few plays, and in the spring of this year I was taken to the Charité hospital because of undernourishment. Arnolt Bronnen was unable to help me substantially out of his earnings as a sales clerk. After twenty-four years in the light of the world I have grown rather thin.

Brecht, letter to Herbert Jhering, October 1922, *Letters*, p. 71.

Foreword

Until now there have been few reliable accounts of Brecht's early years. Franz Xaver Bayerl's research was left unfinished; he died before he could complete his task of collecting material about the genealogy, childhood and youth of the poet and writer. Some of his discoveries were incorporated in Max Högel's study for the series *Lebensbilder aus dem Bayerischen Schwaben* (*Lives from Bavarian Swabia*).[1]

Otherwise, the stories told with almost uniform regularity in biographies and appreciations of Brecht do not really bear serious examination. Brecht himself did not make things easy for his interviewers; he had a good sense of humour, and those who knew him well will doubtless have vivid memories of his pealing laughter. Pestering inquisitors were often treated to preposterous fabrications, which they accepted with equally preposterous naivety. For example, the grotesque and quite implausible account of his military hospital service, with which Brecht regaled Tretyakov, has often been taken at face value and reiterated blithely. In contrast, the posthumously published account by Arnolt Bronnen, together with extracts from their correspondence, does appear to be entirely reliable. It opens in the winter of 1921–2 and is an invaluable account of Brecht's first sojourn in Berlin.[2]

This memoir likewise confines itself to a particular span of years. Despite my lifelong friendship with Brecht, which admittedly was interrupted for nearly quarter of a century, I have concentrated on the years 1918 to 1922. It is only from this period that my diaries have survived. From them one can reconstruct a

---

1. See Bibliography (all footnotes are by the translators).
2. The Tretyakov story is elaborated below (p. 54). Some extracts from Bronnen's memoir are collected in 'Further Perspectives' (pp. 119 and 169–71) (See also Bibliography).

record for the late autumn of 1918 until the winter of 1922–3.
They often serve to date the composition of Brecht's works
beyond all doubt, and they uncover several serious divergences
from the chronology generally accepted by the critics.[3]

From my notes of these years, and from my memories, I
have been able to point to some hitherto unknown works by
Brecht; whether these references will be of any value to scholars
is as yet unclear. However, it is certain, despite the immense
volume of papers preserved in the Brecht Archive, that it still
does not contain his entire oeuvre. It is equally clear that several
important documents must have survived in hitherto inaccessible
private collections. Finally, there are reliable accounts that in a
moment of panic, when Brecht went into exile and was deprived
of his citizenship, a whole laundry-basket stuffed with his manuscripts was shifted from Augsburg to Darmstadt, where it
evidently fell victim to the bombing raids. The very fact that my
remarks have already led to the discovery of a number of lost
manuscripts and publications from Brecht's earliest years must
surely justify my committing to paper all that I know. Even if
fears of irreplaceable losses turn out to be unfounded, there is
perhaps the chance that this book may prompt some important
discoveries.

With regard to quotations from memory, I have been concerned to reproduce, with only very few exceptions, the exact
wording of the lost originals. Where published versions permit a
comparison – this is true also of the quotations from Wedekind
and Nestroy – I have preserved the characteristic deviations of
Brecht's own favourite renderings.

My account is deliberately confined to what I myself
experienced. It is not intended as a scholarly work, nor can it pre-
empt the projected study of the young Brecht which has been
announced by the Suhrkamp publishing house.[4] For both it may
furnish material. It will be the task of literary historians and
biographers to separate the significant from the trivial. The fac-

3. For extracts from Münsterer's diary see pp. 144–6 and 158.
4. This study was never published and has not been identified.

tual information about dates and unfamiliar works may even be of use to the editors of the critical edition of Brecht's complete works.

Munich, January 1963

First Letters   *Urbaal*[1]

I first met Bert Brecht in the autumn of 1917. I was in my last but one year at grammar school in Augsburg; he had just started his first term at college in Munich.

Our ancient Imperial City, which had declined into a provincial backwater, still breathed order and respectability; on public occasions they still put out the flags; but the flower of a generation which had been herded, jubilant and unquestioning, into the raking guns of Flanders lay dead. The war had torn open too many graves. From day to day it was becoming harder to ignore the voices of the pacifists who had fled to Switzerland, or the sickly yellow faces of the scrawny little munition girls from Bobingen, as they scuttled through the market on their days off; and if you walked through the streets in the early morning, before the police had been round, you could still read the verses, scrawled in chalk on the walls:

> We don't fight for the Fatherland,
>   and we don't fight for the Lord.
> We just fight for the wealthy ones,
>   and trample on the poor.

It was a quite different message from the one proclaimed by the 'starched shirts' of the establishment. It hit home with tremendous force and made people think. The shock-waves can be felt in Brecht's work too. In *The Three Soldiers* for example, a children's book of 1931, the same idea returns – the anger has ebbed, but the lesson remains:

> When the fourth long year had come,
> it was clear to everyone,
> the war would cost the poor folks dear,

1. The first version of *Baal*.

and that the rich were only waging war
to fill their coffers even more.[2]

Anyway, for us sixteen year olds the shift from an unquestioning belief in authority towards our own independent judgement had one extremely unfortunate consequence: our obedient
enthusiasm for U-boat commanders and fighter-pilots was appre-
ciably dampened, and there was quite a storm in the staff-room
when the headmaster discovered that some of us had skipped a
patriotic speech by a naval commander in order to read Mörike.
For we were becoming more and more interested in literature,
and had even tried our hands at writing our own poetry –
although we never achieved much more than a thin concoction of
Eichendorff and Goethe, which even a dash of Heine or
Wedekind could do little to enliven. Of course we laughed when
one of our aspiring poets carried the unintentional humour so far
as to describe a potter's work as follows:

> His pots he turns with utmost zeal
> and charming manners grace his wheel.[3]

Generally, however, we took our artistic efforts far too seriously.
Some of them even met with the approval of editors who
published them in the local rags, mercifully omitting our names –
for the original begetters had often been dead for a hundred years
or more.

In the late summer, when I was away near Salzburg, a letter
from Otto Bezold arrived shattering this mood of self-satisfaction:
at a concert in the park in Augsburg he had met a real poet. All
that I knew of this young man at first was that he wrote music and
book reviews and occasionally covered provincial arts events for
local newspapers. I must confess that I had imagined a poet's life
to be far more romantic than that. Nevertheless, I was very
excited at the prospect of meeting him. It was several weeks
before I got the chance. One evening when we were hanging

---

2. For the original German text of all Brecht's poetry quoted by Münsterer, see pp. 176–86 (see p. xii–xiii above for editorial explanation).
3. The humour of the German depends on the dual meaning of 'guter
Ton' ('good clay' or 'good form/manners').

round the city walls in the hope of running into him, our patience was rewarded – I was introduced straight away. Brecht had already read some of my poetry, and after a few minutes small-talk he asked me to visit him in his flat at 2 Bleichstraße and to bring along as many manuscripts as I could.

Next Sunday at about eleven o'clock I donned my most elegant apparel, knotted my finest cravat with a sartorial flourish, pulled on my grey kid-gloves, and given half a chance would have gone brandishing a top-hat too, all for the sake of the bourgeois protocol of Imperial Germany. Brecht captured all this in the poem 'Song to Herr Münsterer' which he later sent me – perhaps one of the earliest examples of the genre of 'lyric portrait' which the American poets were to make their own:

> Beneath his gaze so pure there leered
> a hint of his damnation.
> From a frayed lapel obscenely peered,
> smelling of death, a white carnation.

> Golden hair, it was said,
> his passions could engage;
> but he never deflowered a maid
> under fifteen years of age.

> So long as it worked life was a spree:
> His bluish blood saw to that.
> He'd doff for every pretty tree
> his (peculiarly scruffy) hat.

> The glove he wore of finest grey
> was elegantly grand:
> Only beasts and beauties – they
> felt his naked hand.

The Klaucke suburb, near the Haindl paperworks and the Riedinger balloon factory, was not a part of town I knew. Now I found myself in a network of perfectly straight, parallel streets intersected by others, nearly as straight and even more lifeless. To right and left at regular intervals stood absolutely identical, grey, two-storey houses, each containing four flats. This then was one of those quarters or 'estates' which the factory owners of the nineties had built for their workers and staff. I had never come across anything quite like it and I was appalled at the total absence of any kind of individuality. The house where the Brechts lived, with its walled, concrete yard, compounded the overall impression of aridity and lovelessness.[4] However, it was actually one of the most pleasant in this sorry company: to the south it had a clear view over the old avenue of chestnut trees and the town moat, which lay in the shadow of the old city fortifications, their dark red stone swathed in ivy. There were swans here and punt parties on spring nights, singing, paper lanterns and girls; above them reared the proud silhouette of the Fünfgrat tower and, further on, the 'Dahinab [Down there] steps' wound their precipitous way up to the old town – so-called because Luther is said to have been helped on his flight from the Reichstag with those very words. And all that – the water, walls and white candelabra of the blossoming trees beamed across at the poor drab corner house. In those days Brecht still gratefully acknowledged the romanticism of these surroundings: 'Isn't it just like one of those paintings by Spitzweg?' he said once, looking out of the window as a head of blonde curls appeared at the skylight of a neighbouring house.

The Brecht family lived on the first floor, a model of petit-bourgeois respectability; but I wanted to visit Bert and so I was shown upstairs to the attic where Eugen (or 'our Aigin' as his parents called him) had a room of his own. Those much quoted edicts of his were pinned to the door: visitors were politely requested to come armed with common sense and good ideas, but to make sure they left their prejudices behind – amen! – and there were a few more abrasive sallies as a foretaste of what was to come. The whole text consisted of no more than ten or twelve beautifully formulated little commandments, and breathed the spirit of Lichtenberg or of *Zarathustra*. Nevertheless, this cold shower is said to have had the intended effect of discouraging

4. See pp. 115–20 for other accounts of this environment. Münsterer's family lived in the smarter Maximilianstraße, the main street in the centre of the old town, hence his reaction.

visitors with too little sympathy for wit and originality. Once over the threshold one entered another world. The room was not very large, and it had only one window. The bed was immediately on the right and to the left under the sloping roof there was a makeshift couch. The only other furniture consisted of a simple table, groaning under piles of manuscripts and books, and two or three chairs. The walls were decorated with a couple of pictures by Caspar Neher, and the room was lit by a red paper lantern. Brecht already had company when I arrived: a young girl, rather pale and freckled – but that only enhanced her pretty face. Literary historians know her by the nicknames 'Bi', 'Teddy' or 'Paul Bittersweet'; Brecht's biographers know her as the mother of his first son. Of course I was urged to recite a few of my own poems, two of which pleased Brecht so much that he made copies for himself; but then it was his turn to present some of his own work, which he recited or sang, accompanying himself on the guitar. If I am not mistaken we heard 'Evlyn Roe', 'Ballad of the adventurers' and 'Orge's reply on being sent a soaped noose', evidently all recent compositions. I don't suppose we talked about theatre projects at that stage, but we did find that we shared a common enthusiasm for the talents of both Wedekind and Georg Büchner. I gladly assured him that I would come again as soon as I could.

Not long after, that same winter I think, I went to see Brecht in his Munich lodgings. They were in Paul-Heyse-Straße in the office buildings of the newspaper, *Die Münchner Zeitung*. In the courtyard one had to negotiate a whole succession of steps and staircases leading into the right wing of the building; and then there was a long winding corridor from which, as in a hospital, door upon door opened on to a maze of narrow cells. Of course such a student hostel provided Brecht with a large captive audience, and it was probably here that he started posting a weekly bulletin of aphorisms and sayings in the lavatory – for the general edification of all and sundry. Often he followed the example of the master Karl Valentin and took everyday proverbs, altering them just slightly to give them a new and sometimes quite startling twist: 'He's a chip off the old potato', or 'If you scratch my back, I'll wash your hands.' Sometimes they were bitter little maxims modelled on the sayings of the financier Jéroboam, which had just been published along with Chesterton's *A Defence of Nonsense* in the 'Weiße Blätter' series.[5] A saying like, 'A poor idiot is an idiot, but a rich idiot is rich', could of course be recast along the lines: 'An old ass is an ass, but a young ass is young'. Admittedly, in our efforts to outdo each other, these little adages sometimes strayed rather near the knuckle; but that just showed how well they fitted into the good old German tradition of farce and buffoonery – at this time Brecht owned Fischer's anthology published by Rothbarth. After all, Karl Valentin himself was well known for his promotion of a patent electric nose-picker designed to do away with the effort of picking your nose with your own fingers; and his infamous pub belching scene was a veritable *tour de force* of tastelessness.[6]

After that we saw each other more and more often to talk about our literary projects, either at my place in Maximilianstraße or at Brecht's in Bleichstraße, but Brecht's endless toing and froing between Munich and Augsburg meant there also had to be some correspondence. The two letters which have survived from this period presuppose some quite detailed conversations about Brecht's work on *Baal*, and so surely refute the claim that the play was completed in only three days – even if one is thinking only in terms of the very first draft. One of the letters is dated 'May '18'. Exact dating is problematic, but if my recollection – that this is Brecht's very first written communication to me – is correct, then it must have been sent on Wednesday, 1 May [1918].

Dear Herr Münsterer,

Many thanks for your kind visit; I'm sorry not to have been home. I'd be very glad to see you again down here. Would you have time on Thursday by chance? My comedy-of-sorts, *Baal*, is finished. Have you done anything new? I wish you

5. The malicious maxims *Les Propos de Jéroboam* (from which the following saying is taken) were published by Paul Laffitte, French financier and owner of Les Éditions de la Sirène.
6. For more on this famous Munich comedian see p. 162.

would write to me here in Munich. Have you any theatrical plans?

With regards,

Yours, Bert Brecht   (Letters, p. 41)[7]

Evidently the invitation reached me too late; the second letter, dated 'Sunday, '18', seems to imply this. The mention of a performance of *Samson*, which took place on Monday the 6th, suggests that this one dates from 5 May.

Dear Herr Münsterer,

I very much regret not having heard from you again. What are you doing? How is your *Faust* coming along? I wish you would write to me! People like you and me get their best ideas while writing. – There's quite a lot going on in Munich at the moment. The theatres are doing guest performances. On Monday I'm seeing a private performance of Wedekind's *Samson* that has been suppressed by the SPCA.[8] I now have a (good?) title for Baal: *Baal eats! Baal dances!! Baal is transfigured!!!*

What do you think of it? Have you a better one? Some idea about *Baal*? You should write to me!

Bert Brecht   (*Letters*, p. 42)

It is worth noting that this letter gives 63 Kaulbachstraße as Brecht's address. Evidently he had already moved from the medics' quarter to Schwabing by the beginning of his second term. In future his address was to alternate back and forth between these opposite ends of town.

I was not very taken with the new title, particularly as its implied irony would have been appreciated only by a connoisseur of the Brechtian idiom. I thought the play should be called *Baal*, leave it at that. And in the end that was the title that stuck.

Although I was in on the very beginnings of Brecht's play I

7. See pp. xv–xvi above for list of abbreviated titles.
8. A humorous reference to censorship, which could be evaded by having single 'theatre club' performances.

am not at all sure where he got the name Baal from. Of course
one immediately thinks of associations with the biblical Baal.
However, the word appears as a proper name in several other
contemporary literary works and Brecht certainly had no intention of launching a new myth with his play. The suggestion that
there is a connection with Georg Heym, who at one point refers to
the evil 'God of the Cities' crouching on a tenement block as Baal,
does not seem very convincing to me. Indeed I rather doubt that
Heym, who came from Berlin, played any part at all in the
development of Brecht's lyric poetry, which is so obviously
influenced directly by Verlaine and Rimbaud. In any case,
Heym's name never cropped up in conversation; and the
researches of Dieter Schmidt have established that the poem from
his *Umbra vitae*, along with the one by J. R. Becher, were only
included in the soirée scene of *Baal* during Brecht's revisions for
the complete works some thirty-five years after the real 'first
draft'.[9] Nor can I recall the picture of the 'Syrian Earth-God'
which Brecht is supposed to have prized so highly, and which
most biographers mention as hanging over his bed. The
references to a human skull suggest that these accounts should be
dated to the autumn of 1918 at the earliest; it seems most likely
that they are misinterpretations of the caricatures by Caspar
Neher, which represented, almost life-size in some cases, the
mongoloid wide-browed Verlainesque type of Brecht's hero.

On the occasion of the rather colourless 1926 Berlin adaptation of the play, Brecht published an essay citing an 'original
model for Baal' ('Das Urbild Baals'), a disreputable individual by
the name of Josef K. But that seems a bit questionable when one
remembers that *Baal* started life as a conscious riposte to Johst's
play about Grabbe, *Der Einsame* (*The Lonely One*), which was
performed to some acclaim in the Munich Kammerspiele in
March 1918 (I went to see it myself). Brecht intended to set up a
foil to Johst's fey young poet with his own figure of the rude
wastrel-rhymer who is so clearly derived from the great Verlaine,
and when he came across a copy of Johst's scenario in my library

9. See Bibliography. Schmidt's work, which makes important use of
conversations with Münsterer, was published after this memoir.

he was even going to inscribe it with a note to that effect. Of course the idea of a literary source does not exclude the possibility of a real-life model too. I can only say that Brecht never mentioned such a character to me; on the contrary, once he even raised the question whether, on one particular occasion, Neher or himself had been 'the real Baal'. Given Brecht's fondness for cryptic disguises I should be inclined to dismiss the whole report as deliberate obfuscation. And although Josef K. is described in Brecht's essay as a 'trained mechanic' (and in Feuchtwanger's roman-à-clef *Success* the Brecht-like Kaspar Pröckl is an engineer) this ominous K. might best be read as Keuner, or 'Keiner', that is to say: 'Outis.'[10]

10. This sentence requires some elucidation. Brecht's *Tales of Herr Keuner* (started in the late twenties) contain elements of self-portrait; however, the name Keuner derives from the German 'keiner' ('nobody'). Odysseus tricked the Cyclops by telling Polyphemus his name was 'outis' ('no-man'). See p. 164 for the portrait of Brecht in Lion Feuchtwanger's *Success*.

2

Friends and Family

Almost all Brecht's early friends and several of those he made in later life have remarked on his tremendous personal magnetism. I, for one, was hooked from the start, and would have gone through hell and high water for him. It became a very close friendship. Brecht was two and half years my senior, and I hero-worshipped him; he was an idolized elder brother, the sort one tries to emulate but can never quite live up to. This was not without its dangers: I carelessly swept away all my bourgeois ideals, but still had not laid the proper foundations for an alternative view of the world. Brecht, as the more experienced of the two, often had to check my childish over-enthusiasm, which was so uncompromising and lacking in worldly wisdom that it could not help but provoke offence and hostility. Of course Brecht himself was not above the odd disreputable trick, as for example the notorious episode with his school work proves.[1] Even much later, in 1950, during the rehearsals for *Mother Courage*, he claimed jokingly that his greatest work was not this play, but his own deft forgeries of his father's signature. For it was with these that he had managed to avoid the cadet training corps – which bore the splendid name 'Landsturmriege' ('Home-reserve brigade'), and for which we had to sacrifice two of our free afternoons, and sometimes even Sundays, just to do physical jerks and drill with dummy rifles.

I remember one occasion, when Brecht was predicting the different ways in which his friends would die, he said that I would take a revolver to my forehead. However, later, when the time

1. He was reputed – instead of trying to rub out the teacher's corrections as most schoolchildren might – to have added *more* red marks. That way he could claim that his work must have been marked down unfairly and so persuade the teacher to improve the final mark (a pupil is described as doing this in Brecht's *Flüchtlingsgespräche* (*Refugee Conversations*), *GW*, vol. 14, pp. 1403–4).

had come and that very possibility was staring me in the face, it was he of all people who held me back from my heroic exit and counselled evasion and diplomacy.[2] Brecht had a great influence on his other friends too, if not quite as great as on me, who was by far the youngest of the group. They all looked up to him and respected him as the leader. His oldest friend was George Pfanzelt, known as Orge, a small, enigmatic fellow with a slight limp: the Merck and Mephistopheles of our circle[3] whose smug interjections Brecht always took quite seriously. In those days he was a lowly clerk at the local savings-bank, but he was also exceptionally musical. Brecht thought very highly of some of Pfanzelt's compositions, and he once set one of my own poems. He was probably the only one from whom Brecht could hope for any advice if he got into trouble, and he was always happy to accept his suggestions. The other member of the group who was to be a friend for life was Rudolf Caspar Neher, nicknamed Cas, the son of a schoolteacher. When I first got to know Brecht Neher was away at the front, and so I heard about him only by way of one of Brecht's poems.[4] He is depicted in a melancholy mood, crouched in the trenches at his evening chores of shirt-washing and delousing. In the refrain Brecht has him singing softly:

> ... like a maiden sad,
> the only verse that Caspar had:
> I long for peace to come, and to go home!

Early in the summer of 1918 he did indeed have a longish spell of leave, and he spent the whole time tirelessly painting Baals for

2. It was perhaps the family's military background that prompted Brecht's prediction. Münsterer's diaries suggest, however, that as a young man he several times contemplated suicide. The crisis to which he here refers seems to be traceable to a brief attachment to a married woman; it was on this account that Münsterer left Munich and continued his studies in Vienna.
3. Johann Heinrich Merck (1741–91), himself a writer, was at one time a friend of Goethe's. Some of his traits may have provided material for Goethe's Mephistopheles in *Faust*. See pp. 121–9 for more on these friends.
4. Neher's absence provoked a lively and fascinating correspondence (see pp. 135–6 and *Letters*).

Brecht: Baal with guitar, Baal without, Baal sitting, standing, crouching, in a red jacket, fat and bull-necked, Baal in rags. Caspar himself was a blond giant of a man, with enormous talent. He had a sister, a beautiful, rather quiet girl whom Brecht admired for a time and whom we used to serenade of an evening. There is no connection between the Nehers of Augsburg and the great Carola Neher.[5]

In the last year of the war it was Otto Müller's turn to be called up. Müller, who at Brecht's behest called himself Müller-eisert, was far better off than the rest of us; he had a large, elegant flat of his own in the centre of town, and a rich guardian uncle. I can recall very few of Brecht's other friends from those Augsburg days, with the exception of my own schoolfriend Otto Andreas Bezold who was later to go into politics and become a Minister of State in Bavaria. Other names which crop up in the early diaries are Geyer, Prestel, Seuss and Hartmann. One of these was a ruddy, fresh-faced lad, always laughing; and Hartmann became a particularly useful acquaintance when Brecht was at work on *In the Jungle of Cities* and *Man equals Man* and had got interested in poker and 'Jederaffkannsnicht',[6] for he was the only one of our company who could play cards with any skill as well as enthusiasm.

Of course to be one of Brecht's friends you not only had to have an open mind, but also a good deal of courage, for he challenged every traditional idea of propriety. Even Brecht's tremendous personal charm, however, was powerless when confronted with a dull and unadventurous spirit. So Brecht's handful of fervent supporters found themselves ranged against the closed ranks of his countless enemies. They hated him, thought him a wolf in the fold, a tempter and trouble-maker, and they desperately wanted to do down this bogey of the middle classes. It is hardly surprising that the pillars of bourgeois society should have seen him as a public menace. The story goes (and Kutscher confirms it)[7] that the headmaster of the school where Brecht did

---

5. The actress who played the part of Polly in the first production of *The Threepenny Opera*.

6. Presumably a card game.   7. See Bibliography and pp. 159–60.

his final exams sent a letter warning Munich University in no uncertain terms about his difficult pupil. Even Brecht's outward appearance was not exactly calculated to win him friends. Feuchtwanger for example speaks of downright slovenliness;[8] Frank von Schmutz, one of Brecht's early acquaintances, can still remember his habitually filthy fingernails; another recalls his grubby jacket, which 'would have been unacceptable even in Augsburg's dingiest beer-cellar'. Aside from his chronic tooth-decay, which is the subject of one of the more personal poems in the *Domestic Breviary*,[9] I never really noticed that sort of detail. However, the other day when I was reading Haas,[10] who like Thomas Mann could never come to terms with Brecht's 'monstrous talent', the phrase 'gnomic' reminded me that as long ago as 1918 one of the Augsburg society ladies was always talking about Brecht as 'the gnome'. Of course this had nothing to do with his intellectual leanings, but merely with the fact that the poet's head seemed somehow too large for the rest of his body.

Brecht had been eager to introduce me to his friends – his enemies made their own introductions – and our growing friendship brought me into closer contact with his family too. As is well known, Brecht later came to feel the full force of the biblical saying that a prophet is never recognized in his own country, but not of its supposed corollary: that the most bitter opposition to genius begins at home. Admittedly one could hardly expect Brecht's father to have any particular sympathy for his poet son.[11] He had worked his way up from small beginnings to the position of sales director of the Haindl paperworks. I can still see him now – a typical representative of the solid and respectable petty bourgeoisie, to whom 'bohemianism' or extravagant behaviour of any kind were a positive anathema. Nevertheless, he was neither small-minded nor stupid, as is clear from many of the comments he made, and he was undoubtedly proud that poems by his six-

8. See pp. 163–4.
9. 'Of bad teeth' (*Poems*, p. 75), included in an appendix to the 1922 and 1926 versions of the *Domestic Breviary*.
10. See Bibliography.
11. See also p. 120.

teen-year-old son had already been printed in a respected daily newspaper. Even later, around the time of *Baal*, one can perceive a note of secret admiration when he commented on Eugen's literary efforts: 'Personally I can't stand the stuff, but the youngsters seem to like it.' It was just the sort of judgement he might have passed at a board meeting on some sickly new lavender notepaper – before agreeing to put it into production. One should perhaps go easy on him. When in 1919 he forbade his son to publish *Baal* under his own name, it was doubtless with the intention of keeping open the possibility that the young Brecht might take up a bourgeois profession in later life. The scandal which would almost certainly have ensued upon publication might well have closed that door for ever. It seems likely that it was at his father's instigation that Brecht chose a career-oriented course at university. The fact that he went on to choose medicine can scarcely be attributed to his admiration for Büchner.[12] The subject presented itself quite naturally: it was the only faculty which in time of war enjoyed sufficient prestige for its students to be granted at least a temporary reprieve from military service. Since Brecht was certain from very early on that his future lay in the theatre, he set little store by his medical and scientific training; and there is a grain of truth in his ironic observation that at university he 'learnt to play the guitar' – even if one goes on to restore that wilful omission 'and nothing else'.[13] Brecht only seems to have put in sporadic appearances at medicine lectures right at the beginning and in the winter of 1919. Come 1920 I could not even coax him into the dissection room for the one day of assessments on which the whole term depended. His father was obviously none too pernickety in this department either. Once, when taken to task about what his sons were up to, he explained with a chuckle: 'They're only young once you know, they've got to sow their wild oats.' And he went on paying their fees.

12. The dramatist Georg Büchner (1813–37) was a medical student and later lectured on anatomy. For other explanations of Brecht's subject of study, see p. 140.
13. This is what he claimed in 1922 in a letter to Jhering (see p. xxvii), who had asked for some biographical notes.

Although his father viewed Brecht's scribbling with some scepticism, and doubtless secretly hoped for years to come that his prodigal son would 'settle down', his mother was quite convinced, from the very beginning, of her son's future as a great poet. She dreamt that one day he would be a second Ganghofer, and would consort with kings and princes.[14] With an eye to such elevated company, she must sometimes have felt constrained to reproach the young poet for his less than courtly turns of phrase. The poem 'Utterances of a martyr', which Brecht read to me in the summer of 1918, makes unambiguous reference to just such an argument:

> Me, I play billiards upstairs, underneath the eaves,
> where they hang the washing up to dry out, and to piss.
> Each and every day my poor old mother grieves
> that a grown man can behave like this
>
> And can say such things about the washing – so runs her
>   rebuke –
> thoughts like that should only occur to a sick
>   pornographist.
> But how this prissy language makes me want to puke!
> So I say to my mother: Is it my fault if the washing wants
>   a piss!
>
> Then she says: A thing like that must never pass your lips,
>   it's dirty.
> And I say: But I don't ever put it in my mouth.

And the squabble builds up to the concluding outburst:

> They really shouldn't print that stuff about truth in the
>   prayer book
> if we can't tell it as it is.

14. Ludwig Ganghofer (1855–1920), an extremely popular and prolific author of 'light' fiction; he came from Augsburg and was expelled from the grammar school in 1871–2. He wrote patriotic propaganda during the First World War (see also p. 140).

The rather singular title of 'pornographist' which his mother bestowed upon him evidently made quite an impression, for in the Horst-Wessel pamphlet of 1935 he bequeathed it to Hanns Heinz Ewers.[15]

In 1918, when I became acquainted with this splendid woman, a veritable Frau Aja,[16] she was already seriously ill. During the summer months we would wheel her bath-chair out into the tiny garden so that she could enjoy the brief sunshine as it crept over the walls. We used to sit and chat there occasionally; I think she had a soft spot for me, and was even quite proud that her Eugen had found such a devoted friend and admirer in the son of an officer. In spite of his martyr poem, Brecht respected her and adored her unreservedly: the formidable mother figures of his later plays can perhaps only be fully understood in the light of this unique and precious relationship.

Rather more difficult to discern was the attitude of Brecht's younger brother to the poet's life and work.[17] He was quieter than Brecht, more reserved, more respectable, and was so completely overshadowed by his talented sibling that it took some effort to tease out his own not inconsiderable qualities. Brecht's unpublished poem 'The tree of brotherhood' which, to judge from its whole manner, must date from around 1917, and which made a great impression on me at the time, testifies to the bond between the two. The brothers are compared to two tree trunks springing from a single root and growing up with their branches intertwined. In later years the relationship cooled a little, but in those early days the pair of them had several interests in common. Walter played the guitar as well; and I remember one occasion, when I was waiting for Bert, he sang the 'Lied vom alten König' ('Song of the old king'), a folk ballad not unlike Goethe's 'Thule' of which each verse ended with the refrain:

15. Brecht's polemic about the Nazi 'martyr', 'Die Horst-Wessel-Legende', is directed particularly at Ewers's book, *Horst Wessel: Ein deutsches Schicksal* (*Horst Wessel: A German Destiny*) (see *GW*, vol. 20, pp. 209–19).
16. The name given by Goethe's childhood friends to his mother.
17. Compare pp. 121–3.

The king was so old and grey now,
there was nothing else he could do.

I have never come across this excellent little poem in any
anthology and I rather suspect that it was one of Walter's own.[18]

Sometimes the two brothers would perform Brecht or
Wedekind songs with guitar accompaniment. Their rendition of
Brecht's 'Ballad of the pirates', with two voices and, unusually for
such a solitary instrument, two guitars, was especially poignant.
Such evenings might have managed to convey just a little of the
magic of those carefree days to even our most unsympathetic
adversaries.

18. Brecht's 'Der Geschwisterbaum' has now been published in Walter
Brecht's own memoir (Walter Brecht, pp. 206–9). The other song was
evidently not Walter's but was learnt from one of his father's friends
(ibid., pp. 56–7).

3

Cultural Events   Books

The winter of 1917 and the beginning of the following year brought all sorts of exciting theatrical and cultural events which were to be formative in Brecht's subsequent development. Back in October Munich had hosted the production of the play *Jew Süss* by Lion Feuchtwanger, who was soon to become a much closer acquaintance. Now the Augustenstraße theatre was performing *Vasantasena*, Feuchtwanger's adaptation of Sudraka's *Little Clay Cart*. Like previous authors who had tried their hand at adaptations, Feuchtwanger had taken pains to recast this characteristically Indian play in a European form. The Reclam edition, however, offered a faithful translation of all ten acts, and included an all-important prologue and the political sub-plot which, taken together, opened our eyes to alternatives to the familiar Aristotelian drama. Perhaps this early encounter contributed towards Brecht's development of the theory of 'epic theatre' – which at this stage of course lay far in the future. The 30th of March saw the première of Johst's *Der Einsame* (*The Lonely One*) in the Kammerspiele, the play which was the impetus for Brecht's writing of *Baal*. Brecht was particularly disturbed by a dreadful scene where Johst's hero cheats his mother, a poor washerwoman, out of her hard-earned coppers.

Three weeks earlier to the day, on 9 March, Frank Wedekind had died in hospital. Brecht, who was at the cemetery, later described to me how the funeral service had been repeatedly interrupted by grotesque attempts to film the occasion by the deranged Lautensack.[1] Brecht admired Wedekind all his life, he called his first son Frank in his honour and as late as 1950 he had

1. Heinrich Lautensack (1881–1919), a vagabond Expressionist poet and dramatist, and a great fan of Wedekind. He died in an asylum. For more on Wedekind's funeral and on Brecht's own relationship with the father of this generation of dramatists, see pp. 157–8.

raised with me the possibility of a revival of *Spring Awakening* which had made such an impression on us all those years ago, with Annemarie Seidel in the role of Wendla. Wedekind was one of the most popular playwrights of the day: I remember productions of *Earth-Spirit, Oaha, Dance of Death* and the musical piece *Felix and Galathea*, and then, after the revolution, *Schloß Wetterstein* and *Pandora's Box*, and of course *The Marquis of Keith* directed by Albert Steinrück in the Residenztheater. Brecht must been familiar with Wedekind from very early on, although I am not sure what his father was thinking of when he gave him the complete works in the 1912 Georg Müller edition. Brecht had certainly read it from cover to cover, and the state of his copy by 1918 was nothing if not well-thumbed. For several of Wedekind's songs and broadsheet ballads Brecht composed simple but poignant melodies. The most striking was perhaps his rendition of 'Der blinde Knabe' ('The blind boy'), with its bitter realization:

> The world I do renounce and spurn,
> though well I loved it but of late,
> for while God leaves the just to burn
> the unjust celebrate.

No less impressive was the cry of the cuckoo with its shrill conclusion:

> Mankind enjoys the untold wealth of reason
> and yet becomes a pauper at its hands.

His repertoire included several other Wedekind songs, such as 'Der Gartenturm' ('The garden tower'), which we came across in an old Kammerspiele programme:

> When I was but a child
> many an hour I whiled
> climbing the rooftops high
> to watch the birds fly by.

How high they flew, how free,
birds on the wing, far in the distance.
How high they flew, how free,
birds on the wing, in the winds of spring.

Then there was Gwendolin's song about 'true love' from *Der Stein der Weisen* (*The Sages' Stone*), Alma's song from *König Nicolo* ('Strange are the whims of fortune'), 'Das Lied vom armen Kind' ('The song of the beggar-child'), 'Erdgeist' ('Earth-Spirit'), 'Die Wetterfahne' ('The weather-vane'), which was particularly good for serenades, and 'Galathea', for which Brecht had composed a particularly striking setting: he lingered lovingly over three lines out of each stanza, but raced through the address to the beloved in the second line, 'Galathea, pretty child', at a galloping rate.

There was only one occasion when Brecht and Wedekind actually met and that was when, quite literally, they bumped into each other. Brecht had arrived far too early for one of Wedekind's performances, probably one of the Saturday matinées in the Bonbonnière. The hall was still quite empty save for Wedekind himself. He was evidently suffering from nerves and, still wearing his top-hat, had begun to pace up and down between the rows like a caged animal. Brecht stepped out, probably on purpose, into the path of the oncoming Wedekind – who promptly ran straight into him. 'I do beg your pardon,' he said raising his hat, and steamed on. That at least was Brecht's story, and he was quite pleased with himself for having managed to elicit even this greeting from the great master.

Our discoveries were not, however, confined to the world of literature; the visual arts had exciting things to offer too. In the new Staatsgalerie there were pictures by Van Gogh and Gauguin, Kokoschka's blue-green moonscapes, and a splendid painting by Max Liebermann. It was the gestural quality of this last picture which caught Brecht's imagination: the visible strain of an old woman tugging at an obstinate goat. This was the time too when the Isenheim Altar, that most revolutionary expression of the transition between the medieval and the modern, was on display in the Alte Pinakothek. Brecht, already with an eye for the theatre, especially admired the figure of St John gesturing with his exaggeratedly long crooked finger towards the historic scenes on Golgotha. Not long afterwards we had our first opportunity to see some of Max Beckmann's work. The pictures which had not been included in the official exhibition were housed in an annexe of the Glaspalast, and there we marvelled at the strange, macabre clown and circus scenes which are characteristic of the artist's early period.

The very fact that we young people of Augsburg did not seek our entertainment locally, in our own Swabian metropolis, but in its neighbouring Bavarian rival, begs the question what Augsburg did have to offer. Literary historians have often aired their doubts, not without justification, as to the intellectual opportunities offered by the town. The young Brecht would probably have snorted that Augsburg's greatest intellectual opportunity was the express train to Munich, and he would not have been far wrong. Of course Augsburg did have its own theatre, which staged operettas one after the other, like *Dollarprinzessin* (*The Dollar Princess*) and *Alt-Heidelberg* (*Old Heidelberg*) – later Brecht had quite a set-to with the theatre.[2] The music programme was decent enough, and there are indeed several concert reviews from the autumn of 1917 which are clearly Brecht's handiwork. There was an art gallery, more or less deserted except for Neher with his sketch-book. There was even a literary society; and alongside such innocent guests as Walter von Molo or Jakob Wassermann they occasionally, and with heavy hearts, invited Expressionists like the portly Theodor Däubler. Once, in a fit of twenties radicalism, they even held a poetry reading for that arch-bohemian Joachim Ringelnatz. When all is said and done, however, Augsburg's unique advantage was the handy connection to Munich – a city which had long since been relegated to second place by Berlin but still had life in it and managed to maintain its reputation as the cultural centre of Southern Germany.

Augsburg's glories were glories past. The frontage of the town-hall trumpeted the city's former independence: no prince

2. See pp. 160–2.

nor bishop held sway here. But that breed of royal merchants who in former times had lent the Kaiser money and then torn up the credit notes was now gone for ever. The proud administrative capital of Bavarian Swabia had been reduced to a town of petty officials and traders; and the verb 'fuggern',[3] which had once implied a worldwide trading network, now meant little more than swindling and small-time fraud. For Brecht, those schooldays were like being pickled in a jar,[4] and he observed with regret that he had not succeeded in really broadening the horizons of any of his teachers. The high point of the cultural calendar, he said, was the fair – with its sideshows, panoramas and waxworks. Whatever reservations one may have about such sarcastic remarks, it does remain a devastating conclusion.

Augsburg did have one advantage: an excellent bookshop with a lending section which kept up to date with all the latest publications.[5] There were all sorts of rumours about the proprietor though – he was said to be suffering from a 'social disease', to have kept a hoard of dirty books, or even to have moonlighted as a pimp. Whatever the case, in both of his shops, and especially in the basement in Königsplatz, you could browse and dabble to your heart's content. This was where we discovered Strindberg, beautiful early editions from the Insel collection, Eugen Diederich's 'Renaissance' series, Samuel Fischer, Langen, Müller, and the ubiquitous Kurt Wolff, who swamped the market with a veritable flood of new titles – the 'Jüngste Tag' series, and all those new novels in their bright yellow covers.

I remember during the war how I used to read by the light of a precious little stub of tallow candle till three o'clock in the morning. Then it would get light through my window, which faced east, and had my bed pushed right up against it. Later, in school, we could carry on reading with the book hidden on our laps. At midday it was time to exchange it for another one; and so it went on, day after day, week after week.

3. A verb made from the name of the great German banking family.
4. Münsterer uses the word 'eingeweckt' (bottled up, pickled), quoting Brecht's letter to Jhering (see above, p. xxvii).
5. Steinicke's bookshop and library (see pp. 31–2).

It is unlikely that Brecht had any more comfortable a time of it than me, yet in his early youth he too had somehow ploughed his way through the majority of the available world literature. He was made to wear glasses from very early on, and his comments in *Refugee Conversations* bear witness to his voracious reading habits: Five pfennigs a book – Zola, Casanova with Bayros illustrations (that was the Borngräber edition), Maupassant, Nietzsche, Bleibtreu (that puts me in mind of a bitter but eventually successful campaign to procure *Nana*) – 'If you spend all day with your nose in a book you'll be finished by the time you're nineteen' (that was probably a warning from his mother).[6] In 1916 Brecht made a note that he had rather lost interest in Nietzsche, but was very taken with Spinoza.[7] It is a telling remark: both Lessing and Goethe came round to this abstruse thinker only much later in life.

The series 'Aus fremden Gärten' ('From distant gardens'), edited by Otto Hauser, was a veritable treasure-trove of literary delights. It had everything you could ask for: Chinese literature, French, American, Hebrew, English, Italian, Croatian, Spanish, even Samoyed. As translations they read very well, but were probably not very accurate. Each time another slim volume appeared, malicious critics would observe that the translator, who had already demonstrated his incompetence in ninety-eight languages, had now added to his failures a ninety-ninth – in which he was just as incompetent. It was this series that contained a selection of Kipling's ballads (another was produced by Zeitler), from which Brecht learnt a great deal. But the most sought-after Hauser issues were those devoted to Verlaine, Baudelaire, Walt Whitman and Li T'ai-po. Whatever academics may say about them, we adored them. Whenever I think of Verlaine's 'Sérénade' ('Like a deathly voice from beyond the grave') or of 'le chevalier Malheur', I can still hear Brecht's inflection as he

6. This is a garbled quotation, with running commentary, from *Refugee Conversations* (*GW*, vol. 14, pp. 1411–12); Münsterer omits the sexual thoughts with which Brecht laces this version of his memories. Compare p. 129.
7. On a diary leaf for 21 October 1916 which was in Münsterer's possession, see pp. 130–2.

read Hauser's texts. In comparison, Kalckreuth's translations are flat and alien.

I certainly cannot corroborate the widely held opinion that the young Brecht had little time for contemporary German poetry, and little respect for Rilke in particular. He had a very high regard for *The Book of Hours*, and used also to recite 'The Three Kings', which he had come across in a publisher's catalogue, with real enthusiasm. The same could not be said for Stefan George: here the discrepancy between the weight of form and the paucity of content was all too obvious. Even Theodor Haecker has remarked how ill George's poems stand up to that most telling test of poetic worth: the ability to retain their beauty in translation.[8] The difference is indeed remarkable. Brecht's poetry loses nothing of its brilliance in translation; the French versions of George on the other hand seem banal and trivial.

The year 1918 marks Brecht's discovery of Villon. It is possible that he had come across him earlier by way of Dehmel's versions but we did not discover the magnificent, and more expensive, edition of Klammer's translations until eleven years after it had first appeared. Brecht was delighted, and he loved to recite the 'Ballade de la grosse Margot' and 'Ballade de merci':

> With mallets weighted down with lead
> let's smash their ugly faces in.
> There's nothing to be done or said
> but beg that they forgive my sin.[9]

The immediate impact on Brecht's poetry is clear enough, and one can detect reverberations even many years later. That same summer of 1918 Brecht wrote the poem 'Of François Villon' which is in the *Domestic Breviary*. He experimented with the forms of 'oraison' and 'leçon', and he began to use the title 'ballade' for his own poems, in just the same sense as Villon. The use of 'prayers' and 'rogations' seems to have been quite widespread

8. Haecker was a Christian philosopher. This remark comes from an essay of 1924 about Francis Thompson.

9. Münsterer quotes part of the translation of Villon's *Testament* by Karl Klammer (pseudonym: K. L. Ammer) which Brecht later borrowed verbatim for a song in *The Threepenny Opera*.

at the time. We were familiar, for example, with Stadler's translations of Jammes's *Prières*, of which Brecht's particular favourite
was 'Prière pour aller au paradis avec les ânes', as well as with
several of Verlaine's late and pious poems. I myself had plans for
an entire collection, *A Catholic Prayer-Book: For All Con-
tingencies, However Delicate*. One of the poems which happened to
survive, was published by Döblin some thirty years later.[10]

As with Villon, it was Klammer's translations which gave us
our first taste of Rimbaud, and a double issue of the *Münchner
Blätter* in 1919 provided a further impulse. Our interest in exotic
settings was fuelled by the American Bret Harte and by the Dane
Johannes Vilhelm Jensen, as well as by Kipling. We liked
Claudel, whose *L'Annonce faite à Marie* was staged at the Kammerspiele, and we admired Hamsun and Dostoyevsky too. One of
my own poems captures something of these memories:

> Trotting through the theatre of the sky
> Brothers Karamazov and old Baal go by.

This almost certainly derives from a specific occasion, perhaps
even from one of Brecht's own remarks.[11] Of the Spanish writers
Calderón was our particular favourite, and Brecht also suggested
a connection between his own one-act plays of 1919 and Cervantes's 'entremeses'.

Strangely enough we never became all that closely acquainted
with early English drama, apart from Shakespeare of course. I
personally do not remember the enthusiasm, which Brecht is
supposed to have shared with one of his teachers, for pre-
Shakespearian theatre. At any rate, when I mentioned *Edward II*
to him in 1922 – a play which had made a great impression on me
– it seems that the only Marlowe he then knew was *Dr Faustus*. Of
course this was partly due to the inaccessibility of these works.
Even today, the great Anglo-Saxon dramatic tradition is more or
less inaccessible to the German reader: from Heywood and

---

10. In the journal *Das Goldene Tor*, which Döblin edited.
11. Brecht paired 'Brother Baal and Brother Karamazov' in a very
similar way in a poem called 'Lied von den Seligen' ('Song of the
blessed') (*GW*, vol. 8, p. 57).

Webster to Farquhar and Gay, and ultimately to Synge – to
mention just a few of the names which were to be significant in
Brecht's own development. Of course Bernard Shaw we knew,
loved, and argued long and hard about; and we were absolutely
delighted by Swift, especially by his devastating satire about making Irish babies 'beneficial to the Publick', perhaps the most
bitter pamphlet in the whole of world literature.

Of the German classics Brecht admired Büchner, Grabbe,
Kleist, and Goethe of course, but above all Schiller. Yet I could
never interest him in my own special favourite, Lenz. The fact
that both Grabbe and Kleist had written plays about the
'Hermannsschlacht'[12] gave Brecht the opportunity to compare
their skills: in Kleist he saw the greater and more disciplined
talent, and in Grabbe the spontaneous genius. In Schiller he
admired especially the sinew of the broad dramatic sweep, and
the flawless vaulting of his plays and ballads. Above all it was *Don
Carlos* which he had, 'God knows, always loved', as he once
confessed in a review.[13] If, in this play, Posa is an enigmatic and
ambivalent character, then how much more impenetrable is King
Philip himself! Brecht reckoned that not even Schiller could fully
have understood him. *The Maid of Orleans* was the subject of a
talk he once gave in the Kammerspiele in the early twenties, and
his audience said they had never heard such a beautiful appreciation of Schiller. Brecht was to return to the story of this play on
at least three further occasions. In his later plays, especially *St
Joan of the Stockyards* and *Pointed Heads and Round Heads*, he
incorporated quotations and even whole passages of Schiller and
Goethe in a spirit of parody. Yet I do not believe that this was
conceived as an attack on the classics themselves, but rather on
such characters as Mauler and Eskahler,[14] who erect a grand
cultural façade in order to cover up their own dirty dealings.
Brecht had already used a similar technique in his *Drums in the*

12. The historic battle in AD. 9 in which Arminius, the German chief-
tain, defeated the Romans.
13. *Don Carlos* (15 April 1920) (*GW*, vol. 15, p. 9).
14. Mauler is a character in *St Joan*. Eskahler is an earlier name for the
character Missena in the later, more familiar version, of the play, *Round
Heads and Pointed Heads*.

Night. The words of self-denial which, in the mouth of the dying Friedrich III, testified to his nobility – 'Learn to suffer without complaint' – become bitterly sarcastic when the Balickes try to turn these same words against the returning soldier, Andreas Kragler.[15]

Nor were the minor classics unimportant to him. The young realist Brecht had a sneaking admiration for the magic of Eichendorff's *Memoirs of a Good-For-Nothing*; indeed he even ascribes a 'philosophy' to this widely romantic tale. In his youth it seems that Hebbel too was a source of inspiration: on a page of his diary he remarked, 'I can write, I can write plays, better than Hebbel, wilder than Wedekind.'[16] But the pointed criticisms he expressed in a review of *Judith* for the newspaper *Der Volkswille* show that he very soon modified his high opinion of Hebbel; and it was quite possibly the sobering influence of Nestroy's parody which helped to dampen his enthusiasm. Brecht even wrote a Bavarian dialect version of the crushing monologue with which Nestroy lays bare the braggadocio of Hebbel's posturing Horribilicribrifax:[17] 'I'm that hard, me, I'd like to have a scrap wi' m'sel. Then we'd soon see who comes off best, me or me!' This may well have served as a warning to Brecht against the perils of vainglory which lurked in his own *Baal*.

So these were the books we read in beautifully printed and handsomely bound volumes from Steinicke's bookshop and lending library. A little further up the road, still in Heiligkreuz Gasse, there was another little library which provided young Mr Melcher with the means to eke out a pretty miserable existence. It was to this one cluttered room that, according to reliable sources, Brecht would regularly sneak off for his diet of pulp fiction and detective novels. Whether he learnt his craft from such books or whether he found them genuinely entertaining, I

15. Friedrich III is not here a literary figure; these words are popularly accredited to the historical Kaiser who briefly (in 1888) preceded Wilhelm II, his eldest son.
16. This remark comes from the single diary sheet (October 1916) in Münsterer's possession.
17. Münsterer is referring to Holofernes in Hebbel's play *Judith* (see also p. 161).

do not know; he never discussed them with me. Once, however, he gave me a full and lively account of Chesterton's wonderful story 'The Blue Cross', from _The Innocence of Father Brown_ – but that is the best of all his tales, and could almost be classed as 'high art'.

It was, however, with the books we read in our childhood that we really plumbed the depths. I remember _Captain Mors, the Flying Pirate_ who even plundered the Pyramids, but later came to a sticky end when, pawed by countless excited children, his spine finally disintegrated and all his pages fell out. My friend Lupy and I, one summer in Dieuze, gobbled our way through _Captain Mors_ and heaps of damsons in a hay-barn where we were supposed to be selling the fruit. A better read by far was _The Path to Happiness_ by the author of _The Wild Rose_, Karl May himself. This tale was serialized in about a hundred parts, each with a gaudy cover illustration. There were gypsy girls buried at the dead of night, white-slave traders with underground dungeons crammed with hoards of women, Wagnerian operas, and then, travelling incognito and beset with dangers, King Ludwig of Bavaria and his secret detective Wurzelsepp, who spoke in such an incomprehensibly Tyrolean dialect. Brecht's eyes lit up at the exploits of _Bandit Fetzer_ [literally: tearer] too, who was, as it happens, a real historical figure: he owed his name to the horrible way he dismembered his victims. We knew a kitchen-maid in Bleichstraße who had a subscription to _Fetzer_ and she passed on each issue, to slake our thirst for knowledge. Even years later Brecht still enjoyed recounting the following stirring episode. Against her will the bandit's beloved is to be married off by her matchmaking father to a decrepit but wealthy lecher. On the eve of the wedding the bandits surround the house, their chief dices with death and leaps up the drainpipe, swings through the girl's window, and carries off his trembling booty. And now comes the part where even the hardened young proles of Hettenbach all listened with bated breath: 'The bandit-chief Fetzer assured himself that his bride was still a virgin. Behold, she was! And all the bandits, hard men though they were, wept tears of emotion.' Was it not perhaps a distant memory of this tale that provided the stimulus for the song of 'Pirate Jenny' in *The Threepenny Opera*, with its telling subtitle: 'Fantasies of a Kitchen-Maid'?

Almost all of these books left some mark on Brecht's writing. There are quite unmistakable traces of Villon, say, or of Rimbaud, in 'Of the drowned maiden' or 'The ship', and occasionally, as in *In the Jungle of Cities*, Brecht quotes entire phrases word for word. It was this practice which led to the first charges of plagiarism, charges which were to dog Brecht for the rest of his life. The witch-hunt reached a climax when the author of the *Domestic Breviary* was asked to judge a poetry competition, and managed to offend some four hundred aspiring poets. They went so far as to assert that the name of Brecht's friend and the dedicatee of *Baal*, George Pfanzelt, had been stolen from Georg Queri's *Egidius Pfanzelter*.[18] Even my own comments in Brecht's defence were turned and used against him by some minor literary journal. Although the charges were laughable, it was only with the support of Bernhard Guillemin and Kurt Müno that the editors were prevailed upon to print the correction I had written. The hacks kept at it right up to *Puntila*. Today, at last, everybody recognizes that it was Brecht's painstaking literary apprenticeship – his conscious development and continual reassessment of tradition – which means that now, more than any other modernist, he may rank as a classic.[19]

While on the subject of Brecht's literary antecedents we must not ignore the role which the ancients played, especially the Roman authors; but there is also one book of quite unique significance which must be taken into account. In response to a questionnaire about which work had made the strongest impression on him, Brecht replied, with the terse humour of a true Berliner: 'Don't laugh: the Bible.' That may have been a joke, and many people understood it as such. However, the many textual and linguistic echos of the Bible in Brecht's work make it clear that he knew the Luther version extremely well. In addition, Brecht

18. Queri (1879–1919), Bavarian journalist and humorist, author of *Die weltlichen Gesänge des Pfanzelter Gidi von Polykarpszell* (1909) (*The Temporal Hymns of Egidius Pfanzelter of Polykarpszell*).
19. On the issue of plagiarism, see also p. 167.

furnished wonderful commentaries on bits of the Old and New Testaments, the most memorable being his notes on the wild and barbarous books of Samuel, which must be in his diaries.

What is more, he took from the Psalms not only the name but also the form for his own poetry. He tried his hand at 'gospels' too – or that is how he described the poems 'Of swimming in lakes and rivers' and 'Of climbing in trees', and one could find at least a couple more examples; in his *Pocket Breviary* he even mimicked the two-column format and used India paper like the Württemberg biblical society.[20] The Catholic and Protestant hymn and prayer books played their part too in the development of his poetry: the Protestant influence is most apparent in his 'liturgies' and 'chorales', the Catholic in his 'rogations' and in the many, often ironic references to the cult of the Virgin. Of course he experienced it all himself when, on a couple of occasions, and then strictly for the benefit of the ladies, I dragged him off to May devotions in the cathedral. The dim, high vault, the flickering candlelight and the soft chanting all had quite an effect on Brecht: Ziffel mentions these occasions,[21] and in Yvette's song in *Mother Courage* we catch another glimpse:

After May devotions,
there came more worldly notions.

In context it is of course an anachronism, for that form of popular piety emerged only towards the end of the seventeenth century and was therefore still unknown during the Thirty Years War.

20. In the *Domestic Breviary* these two poems are actually called 'devotional exercises' ('Exerzitien', not 'Evangelien'). The *Pocket Breviary* (*Taschenpostille*), published privately by Brecht in 1926, was an early version of the *Domestic Breviary* (*Hauspostille*), published in 1927.
21. In *Refugee Conversations*, *GW*, vol. 14, p. 1412.

Loving   Living

I cannot remember very many details of that first year of
friendship with Brecht. But the one thing that must have struck
everyone who came into contact with him was that singular combination of bashful naivety and quite outrageous impudence,
which were all part and parcel of his magnetic charm, and a
continual source of fascination to his friends. I remember one
incident at a concert in the park. In the warm weather these
concerts were held outside, and you could stroll through the
gardens while they played: the ideal opportunity for a bit of
philandering and foolery. However, when the nineteen-year-old
Brecht's attention was attracted by a member of the opposite sex
he was so overcome with adolescent embarrassment that he did
not dare to approach her himself. A younger friend was delegated
to do the business, and he took the matter in hand with the easy
grace of a practised Don Juan. Friendly relations were
established, and before long the couple were off skating together
– 'arm in arm', as Brecht recalls in *Refugee Conversations*, where
the character of Ziffel sheds light on many of the secrets of
this early love affair.[1] The course of true love was not without its
moments of jealousy however, as we can see from one of Brecht's
favourite songs of those days:

> Teddy says she simply could not ever be so proud,
> she'd rather have another kiss if that's allowed.
> Gentlemen, there's more to that than meets the eye!
> Forget it: no one lets bliss pass them by.

> Teddy says there's nothing in a little bit of fun,
> so long as it's in public surely no harm's done.
> Gentlemen, there's more to that than meets the eye!
> Forget it: no one lets bliss pass them by.

1. See pp. 133–4 for Ziffel's version and for more elucidation of the
following paragraphs.

There is also a factual basis to that splendid little anecdote of Ziffel's which provokes Kalle's 'Now, that's what I call a sense of responsibility!' One day, some six months later, we were sitting in Café Stephanie when Brecht repeated verbatim the self-same lecture with which Otto Müller had originally tried to impress on him the importance of 'practice' and 'experience'. What is more, I imagine the youth of Augsburg paid very careful attention to the really rather embarrassing 'accident' in which an otherwise highly respectable lady was severely compromised, and which was at the time a source both of public amusement and dismay.

In the frowsty atmosphere of Augsburg, Brecht's many heroic pranks earned him the reputation for being quite irredeemably degenerate. Some of them I witnessed myself, but most of them I have long since forgotten. There are several stories which are quite in keeping with the general mood: that on Sundays we used to perch on the railings at Schwalbeneck and taunt the good citizens as they passed, or that once, when he had a stiff neck and wanted to talk to a girlfriend up at a second-floor window, he just lay flat on his back in the middle of the street. When they removed the statues of the great poets from the entrance to the Augsburg theatre – in order to melt them down for artillery – Brecht went and stood in one of the empty niches. There is a photograph which shows him just to the right of the doorway, as the new Friedrich von Schiller. The following contretemps from his school-days was told by Brecht himself. One evening at about midnight when he was just emerging from a public house he was waylaid by his form-master and they had this little conversation: 'Well, well, what have we been up to at this time of night, Brecht, m' young lad?' 'I've been to see my uncle, sir.' 'Well, well, well! And what, may I ask, do you have in that bag, Brecht?' 'My guitar, sir.' 'Well, well! Your guitar! And what do you need with your guitar when you're visiting your uncle then, young man?' 'Well, you see, I had to go and play for my uncle, sir!' 'Well, well, well! So you've been playing for your uncle have you, Brecht? But . . . didn't I just see you coming out of that public house?!' 'This public house here, sir? Yes, I had to relieve myself, sir!' 'Well, well! So you've been answering a call of nature in the public house, with your guitar! I see. Well now, young lad, you just get along home now, and sharpish!' 'Yes sir, but first of all I must go to my grandad's . . . you see, I've promised to play for him too' – or at least that's what Brecht claims he replied.

That final riposte may well be a fabrication, but the anecdote still demonstrates that this precocious young schoolboy met with at least some sympathy – and not solely from splendid old Father Romuald who used to teach part-time at the grammar school and who saved Brecht from expulsion.[2] Brecht himself later told me that one of his masters carefully cut out and kept all his poems from newspapers and magazines. Perhaps he did manage, after all, to broaden the horizons of some of his teachers.

His behaviour was an expression of his rebellious and obstreperous nature, although of course not every outburst was equally productive. It might, for example, have been far less time-consuming for Brecht just to show the railway guard his ticket, rather than complain about the inconvenience and argue with him for an hour. Equally, in the cinema it would have been more sensible to ignore the opening credits, rather than to express his disapproval with a chorus of boos and whistles. What is more, after the collapse of the Bavarian Soviet Republic, even quite harmless expressions of doubt about the established order and its representatives could turn out to be pretty dangerous. Once, when a military band struck up, all decked out in their helmets and combat uniform, Brecht registered his amusement to a friend and was summarily arrested and led off. In the event he was back, unharmed, within the hour; but that was a lucky escape. For if my diary notes are correct, that Brecht had been harbouring Brehm (the revolutionary commander of Augsburg) when he was on the run,[3] then, in those perilous days, a little affair like that could all too easily have become a matter of life and death. All in all, we well knew how to stand up for ourselves; and the three soldiers in Brecht's book for children would probably have had no cause to shoot us for excessive obedience![4] My notes mention one

2. See p. 140.
3. i.e. Georg Prem (see pp. 147–9).
4. In Brecht's *The Three Soldiers*, the three survivors of the 1914–18 war

dispute with a priest, for example, which had been provoked by some disparaging remark or other, and which then dragged on for weeks.

Of course it is impossible to construct a coherent picture of the young Brecht from such scattered and fragmentary evidence. His future biographers will need to have substantial recourse to the material in *Refugee Conversations*, the only genuinely autobiographical source which has as yet been published. He entrusted the real 'splendour and filth of his soul' to his diaries,[5] which he mostly kept on yellowish loose leaves of cheap, poor-quality paper. They have probably not survived in full. Judging by the passages which Brecht read aloud to me all those years ago, they must be a rich source, of similar importance to the celebrated diaries of Hebbel – and linguistically far superior. Many of Brecht's observations about his contemporaries must, of course, be taken with a pinch of salt; he was often shockingly harsh and unjust. 'He's a rogue and a scoundrel, but I like his woman', was one of his milder remarks.[6] Later on he often toned such comments down, and even became a good friend to the people he had previously condemned.

ignore the ceasefire and resolve to shoot everyone who won't resist the status quo.

5. A reference to a remark Heinrich von Kleist made about his play *Penthesilea*.

6. In an earlier typescript sketch preserved amongst his papers, Münsterer claims that this remark refers to Lion Feuchtwanger.

Early Work   Early Theory

Of course these detailed reminiscences of Brecht's sheltered and fundamentally middle-class upbringing will be of little interest to literary historians; they will be more eager to hear about his earliest poetic work. The few poems which were actually published during the war years were those which best accorded with the contemporary climate. Some of his contributions to the school-magazine *Die Ernte* and to the *Erzähler*, the literary supplement of the *Augsburger Neueste Nachrichten*, display an unqualified First World War patriotism. One of his poems was even used on a postcard to make propaganda for the war effort. Other works, however, display a quite different emphasis. 'Being a mother in times like these', 'A German springtime prayer', 'Hans Lody', and 'The fields of Belgium' are examples of the latter. Then there is the pious 'Easter legend' dedicated to the orphans, with its image of the blossom springing from the seed of the crown of thorns:

> They tore the crown
> of thorns from his hair,
> and laid him down
> without a prayer.

> When they came to the burial ground
> the next night, tired and worn,
> lo, on the mound,
> flowers had sprung from the thorn.

And 'Modern legend' brings out the suffering which unites victor and vanquished – although not yet with any of the ironic rhetoric of the later 'Song of the water-wheel':

> Late into the night, choirs
> sang in the telegraph wires

of those who had died in battle.
Then it fell silent, friend and foe both slept.
Only the mothers wept
On this side – and on that.

It is difficult to arrive at a satisfactory interpretation of the remarkable poem, 'Tsingtau soldier' for the simple reason that the version printed in the *Erzähler* is disfigured by substantial and probably distorting editorial interventions. Nevertheless, Brecht still thought it significant even years later.

The most poignant of all Brecht's early poems which deal with contemporary events has unfortunately never been published. It was called 'Mothers of the missing' and it tells of how there is always an empty chair kept for the soldier who has not returned; the family wait in patient expectation of one who is, in fact, long since dead.[1]

The rest of Brecht's not insubstantial output from his schooldays has presumably, but for scattered fragments, also been lost. In the course of our friendship Brecht showed me some old works which he could now dismiss with a laugh, but also a handful which still meant rather more to him. Many of his early rhymes are about himself. Perhaps the earliest of all describes his annual excursion to purchase a hat:

Every year in the month of May
Bert Brecht goes out to buy a hat,
carries it home and that is that.

For he never put it on. Instead he consigned it to a cupboard along with all the other hats he had never worn, for it was the fashion in the Brecht clique to go hatless. Rather more engaging was a serenade dating from about 1916, which he was still singing in 1919:

Only the moon and the cats are out,
The girls are safe in slumberland.
In the market-place there's someone about:
Bert Brecht, with his lamp in his hand.

1. 'Mütter Vermißter' was subsequently published (*GW*, vol. 8, p. 15).

One particularly striking poem from about 1917 or 1918, with the Wild West atmosphere of Postl-Sealsfield,[2] tells how Brecht is about to be hanged. In the nick of time – or is it just too late? – a man rushes up with the joyous news: 'Bert Brecht, you've won the Nobel Prize!' – in those days it used to be pronounced with the stress on the 'o', and not 'No-belle' as it is now. There is another early poem which has remained with me all these years. Brecht was fond of performing it on his guitar, and it gives a good picture of the allure of Augsburg's *enfant terrible*. The first verse tells how he used to take on the children at their games 'on the bewitching carousels', but then come the telling verses:

When I go to join the better set
and tell them things that no one else yet knows,
they stare at me till I begin to sweat,
and sweating's not the thing with folks like those.
They look at one another, start to laugh,
and then remark just like my mother does:
he's quite a different sort, he's quite a different sort,
he's quite a different sort of man from us.

And one day when I get to heaven's gate,
and I will get there, you just mark me this,
all those pious souls will remonstrate:
He's all we need for our Elysian bliss!
They'll look at one another, start to laugh,
and then remark just like my mother does:
he's quite a different sort, he's quite a different sort,
he's quite a different sort of man from us.

Perhaps one can distinguish another group of early writings which consisted of a sort of nature poetry. Max Hohenester[3] mentions a series of seasonal elegies, and praises one especially which bore the title of the later drama, 'Summer Symphony'.

2. Charles Sealsfield was the pseudonym of Karl Anton Postl (1793–1864), a priest who fled to America and made a successful career as a journalist and novelist.
3. See Bibliography.

Brecht read me an extract once, but neither of us could muster any enthusiasm for its sentimental tone. As far as I can remember, the elegies were composed in rhyming lines of varying lengths rather like the war poems – a form which crops up again and for the last time in the 'Song of the vulture tree' of 1918, and which requires a particular style of delivery. As a rule Brecht used to read the long lines very quickly with a clear break at the end, so that they matched the short lines and so that the rhyme was emphasized.

I was considerably more taken by another poem in the same style dedicated to the historic flight by Chavez, partly because of the novel subject-matter. I may be wrong, but I think I came across it as an anonymous newspaper contribution long before I ever knew Brecht, but for all my efforts I have never been able to trace the publication. Today the event which inspired the poem is all but forgotten. It took place in those legendary pioneering days when aeroplanes were still equipped with wooden propellers driven by leather belts. Aviators and enthusiasts had assembled from the four corners of the earth, their goal: the first flight over the Alps. The craft, primitive monoplanes – 'airplanes' we proudly called them – stood waiting in their hangers, the men camped out in tents: the French, the Germans, the English, Chavez the Mexican, Belgians, Russians. For days on end the rains beat down, the wind howled, and it was bitterly cold. The airmen stared up at the lowering skies, day after day, and no one dared to risk the flight. Then suddenly Chavez starts the engine – in those days you had to turn the propeller by hand, like crank-starting an old motor-car – he leaps aboard and the aeroplane starts rolling, it lifts off, climbs and climbs, the mountains fall away beneath the banks of cloud. Chavez flies on, up and up: the Alps are conquered. The crowd starts cheering as the machine turns for home and begins its descent; but then, in the midst of the rejoicing, it comes crashing to earth, it shatters and buries Chavez, the conqueror, in its wreckage. As far as I remember this very long poem was in fact a sort of elegy to flying in which the drama of events played little part. Still, the subject-matter points forward to the later chorale and learning play about the flights of Lindbergh and Nungesser.[4]

Of the early poems which have been published since Brecht's death, amongst his favourites in 1917 were the 'Little song' about the harmlessness of alcohol and the 'Philosophical dance' – in which the word 'gracefully' must be stressed on the last syllable:[5]

> We never danced more gracefully
> than over the graves of death.
> God always pipes most prettily
> with our very last breath.

It was once quite eerie when Brecht once stepped out on to the balcony from Otto Müller's darkened room, and there in the pale moonlight croaked and strummed the song of the mortuary woman Litje Pu:

> Litje Pu works hard as she's able
> in the mortuary at the laying-out table,
> scrubs the filthy corpses down
> so they're clean when they go in the ground,
> washes you clean as the day you were born . . .

As pure as man first comes into this life so he shall depart it.

Brecht often performed the 'Ballad of chastity', written in 1918 and taken up into the one-act play *The Wedding* in 1919. Another favourite was the similarly slanted folksong about the chaste youth and the chaste maid who join forces 'against the evil

---

4. There are two poems in *GW* which refer to Chavez's flight: 'Aus keinem anderen Grund' ('For no other reason') and 'Bericht von einer mißlungenen Expedition' ('Report of an unsuccessful expedition'), vol. 8, pp. 57–9 and 98–9. Neither of them accord with Münsterer's description. Münsterer himself wrote a poem named after that other aviator, 'Nungesser' (*Mancher Mann*, pp. 60–1).

5. Münsterer demonstrates the metre by spelling the German trisyllable 'Grazie' (grace) as 'Grazih', with the emphasis on the '-ih'. In the last line of this strophe Brecht puns on the idiom 'auf dem letzten Loch pfeifen', to pipe on the last hole (after which there are no more notes), which means: to be close to ruin or death. Here 'the last hole' could also be the grave.

foe', which had a similar twist. Here the concluding verse falls out rather differently from the ballad:

> The chaste young maid gave birth.
> As for the youth? Well he'll
> be over the hills and far away
> in search of his ideal.

Popular hits were parodied too. In one, it is not the spurned wife who appears to the faithless Heinrich on his wedding night, but rather the ghost of his favourite dog, who magnanimously assures him of absolution. A whole host of trivia, mostly four-liners, proclaimed Brecht's unbounded delight in vulgarity. It is simply part of the artist's make-up – look what painters like Giulio Romano and Félicien Rops got away with, or writers like Bürger, Hoffmann and Maupassant! Some of this has survived in *Urbaal*: 'Praise to the Virgin in the wide skies' or 'If a woman has big hips'. But most of it, like 'For what does a wench want with brains', or the verses about the old fiddles, is presumably lost. Sometimes his cheeky off-the-cuff rhymes were even quite witty. After surveying the park's 'facilities', Brecht came out with:

> You cannot know
> until you've been,
> Ludwig's nicest room
> was his latrine.[6]

That was perhaps the starting-point for Orge's song in *Baal*. One day when Otto Bezold had concocted the following lines:

> He spied a lass,
> his thoughts were not exactly chivalrous
> he felt her ass,

Brecht immediately countered:

> and now our song is getting frivolous

6. The concert hall and pavilion in Augsburg's town park was called the Ludwigsbau ('Ludwig's building').

That became one of our catch-phrases, and for a while we used it to bring any risqué conversation to a close.

Brecht thought only a very few of these early poems worthy of inclusion in the *Domestic Breviary*, although some of them are actually not bad at all. When I try to organize them chronologically I come up with something like the following: 'Song of the Fort Donald railroad gang' and probably 'Mazeppa' date from 1916; 'Of the sinners in hell', 'Orge's reply' and 'Of the friendliness of the world' from 1917 at the latest; 'Ballad of the adventurers' from summer or autumn 1917; 'Death in the forest' from the spring of 1918; and 'Of François Villon' and 'Ballad of the pirates' from the same summer. In the case of 'Of Cortez's men' I am not so sure; that was probably not written until 1919. As for dramatic sketches from these early years, there is one mention of an *Alexanderzug* (*Alexander's Campaign*), for which Curtius Rufus is the only likely source. I imagine Brecht's version was most concerned with the idea of straying further and further into a boundless wilderness, and it probably gave great weight to the philosopher's wonderful speech about the distant Greek homeland, which is said almost to have provoked a mutiny. On one occasion, in 1917 or spring 1918 – the notes which I kept from the autumn onwards do not help here – Brecht and I discussed his plan for a play about Quintus Fabius Maximus. It was to have had some relevance to contemporary events which now escapes me. Then, from April to June 1918, came his first major achievement, the first draft of *Baal*.

In the light of Brecht's later development one cannot help wondering what he thought about philosophy and about the theory of art at this early stage. A conclusive answer is probably impossible even for the most assiduous scholar of the young Brecht. Questions like that take no account of the zest and capriciousness of youth, in which it is possible to admire both Cesare Borgia and St Francis at one and the same time.

Nevertheless, if we confine ourselves to the works which Brecht himself thought important, there is an unmistakable undercurrent which leads us dangerously close to nihilism or existentialism. Some of the poems are extremely pessimistic:

especially the 1917 'Ballad of the adventurers', who should have stayed 'with their mothers who nursed them as babies', and who 'sometimes dream of a little field / with the blue sky overhead, and nothing else'.

Another is 'Evlyn Roe', with its desolate philosophy that salvation can be bought only at a price which puts salvation itself quite out of reach, and which would leave one eternally cast out of both heaven and hell. However, such moments of resigned superiority or of downtrodden despondency are few and far between. Not until the later 'Song of the smoke' does a similar pessimism re-emerge. Once he had rejected all transcendental values, it was only Brecht's tremendous vitality, hunger for experience and lust for life which preserved him. He always used to contend that the value of a poem should be weighed against the value of a piece of cake or an apple – and it was not always the poem that came off best. The value of the poem lay in its 'usefulness', he said, and he was determined that his own life should become his most important work of art, greater than all his literature. One of the statements most revealing of the young Brecht's attitude is a poem from *Urbaal*, later replaced by the ballad 'Of the drowned maiden' – admittedly a more appropriate choice in the context. The earlier poem is called 'The song of the cloud of the night':

> My heart is sad like the cloud of the night
> and homeless too, oh woe!
> The clouds in the sky over tree and field,
> they know not why it's so.
> Theirs is a wide and boundless world.
>
> My heart is wild like the cloud of the night
> and yearning too, oh woe!
> It wants to embrace the whole wide sky,
> and knows not why it's so.
> The cloud of night and the wind alone on high.

In this poem there is still a terrible rift between the urge to be one with the universe and the total inability to perceive a goal or any meaning. Just one year later, however, the lust for life becomes so overwhelming that such problems of existence seem quite paltry:

The question whether God exists up there
while there's a Baal, he couldn't care a jot,
however, Baal's most pressing earthly care
is whether there is wine enough or not.

The philosophy of these lines is that only the earthbound and animal instinct are of any value. One cannot simply dismiss the importance of this for Brecht by pointing out that he himself never actually lived in this way, or by suggesting that this is not, after all, a statement of the author's creed but simply a portrayal of the world of Baal. For in those days Baal's 'Chorale' was the song he performed most often, and it represents the very essence of Brecht's thought at that time.

His commitment to animalism coloured his view of art too. We indulged in heated debates as to whether intellect was not entirely inimical to artistic creativity. It all seemed quite straightforward in the visual arts; Brecht was happy to argue that a good painter simply 'has to be stupid'. His adherence to the idea that reason must be subordinated to instinct might, on the surface, appear to derive from the chthonic ideas of Alfred Schuler; we even equated intellectualism and the Jewish mind as Schuler had done, although we never fell prey to his anti-Semitism. But in fact there was no connection. Right up until his death in 1923, Schuler's ideas were more or less unknown outside his little circle of Swabian 'esotericists'. Much later they reached a wider audience through the work of Ludwig Klages, who took them up and developed them.[7] I do not think Brecht ever encountered Schuler's work, nor indeed any of the remnants of that bohemian Munich scene, who went on celebrating memories of the golden age of Wahnmoching in Fuhrmann's overgrown garden and the 'Orient'.[8]

7. Klages (1872–1956) edited the fragmentary papers of Schuler (1856–1923) after the latter's death. Schuler opposed progress and humanity, and urged the reawakening of a pre-historic principle.
8. 'Wahnmoching' was a nickname for Schwabing, the artists' quarter of

Despite his conviction that the instinctive and irrational were
of vital importance in all literary production, Brecht was still very
aware of the importance of the writer's craft and intellectual
skills. In November 1918, for example, he demonstrated the art-
ful construction of his 'Ballad of the pirates', in which he conjures
the skies and the sea like a maestro of the theatre, and lets darkness fall upon the scene so that in the final stanza, in a moment of
clarity, the reef comes looming out of the black. In other words,
in the midst of this hymn to an untrammelled outlaw existence,
he was using rigorously intellectual methods of composition. His
later entirely contradictory assertion of the primacy of the intellect, when he elevated the work of the poet to the status of a
skilful alchemy, indeed a science, thus represents a necessary, if
excessive, correction to his earlier theory – which was in any case
always refuted by his creative practice.

Of course a young writer in the making cannot avoid a dialogue with the currents of contemporary literature. So it was little
more than a jest on Brecht's part when, years later, in response to
a young researcher's query about his attitude to Naturalism, Sym-
bolism, Impressionism and Expressionism, the great man replied:
'In Augsburg? You must be joking!' In Brecht's circle we
certainly discussed such things; and anyone with any interest in
literature, even in Augsburg, was practically force-fed with that
second generation of Expressionists – thanks to the energies of the
publisher Kurt Wolff. So of course we knew Werfel's collection
of poems *Der Weltfreund* (*The Philanthropist*) and *Der Große Alea*,
and the works of Hasenclever. These were the writers who set the
tone, these were the ones whose challenge we had to meet, whom
we had to emulate, or overcome.

Brecht's attitude to Expressionism is evidently a matter for
debate even today. Part of the problem is finding an adequate
definition of 'Expressionism' as a literary movement, since it is
by no means just an etymological question of translating it as the
'art of expressing'. The very vagueness makes it possible for

Munich. Münsterer must be referring to the Pension Fürmann at 57
Belgradstraße, which had been a popular refuge and meeting-place for
penniless bohemians.

Schondorff to include a play by Wedekind in his anthology, as an early representative of Expressionist drama, whereas Karl Otten's selection goes right up to Brecht's *Baal*.[9] In purely formal terms, there are perceptible traces of the Expressionist style in Brecht's early work. We come across typical Expressionist attitudes, themes and stock characters in an oratorio which probably dates from about 1916. It portrays the rejection of the poetic genius by society and his final destruction by the hand of God. The characters are 'He', 'His Woman', 'The Youth', and 'The Mother'. At the end we hear the voice of God, calling out from the darkness:

> The tree in the grip of my storm truly feels its roots, and even when it is dead it must blossom still, for it can do no other. All things abide with you when you are blind and you cannot know that they are there! Yet I have illuminated you so that you may shed light on all things. Now you must die, for it is your desert. You have always served me and even your defeats were triumphs for me.

> HE: Lord, now I know you, for it has fallen quiet within my soul. [*Door and window are flung open upon an azure night; a distant sound of singing hangs on the air.*]

> How can it be that the night is singing? And the tree and the rooftops and the rafters sing too. I am filled with turmoil, as if there were a world within me – and yet I am but a grain of dust which you have filled with your spirit, so that its feeble wits may forget its insignificance, and that it may dare to create a world of its own! Let me be still, for those who but speak may not hear.

> [*A chorus of harmonious voices begins to sing a requiem –* HE *staggers out into the night, arms aloft. – Voices without words swell to fill the empty and darkening stage.*]

If we compare the conclusion of the oratorio with the last scene of *Baal*, the unmistakable shift in attitude becomes apparent. In the

9. See *Deutsches Theater des Expressionismus*, edited by Joachim Schondorff (Munich, 1962) and *Schrei und Bekenntnis: Expressionistisches Theater*, edited by Karl Otten (Darmstadt, 1959).

first, the protagonist stumbles headlong from the stage with his arms aloft in ecstasy – the very essence of Expressionism; in the second play, Baal, a prisoner of this earthly world, crawls off like an animal, to curl up and die in the undergrowth. If that early date for the draft of the oratorio is correct – the manuscript, which Brecht described as an old work, was given to a musically gifted student as the libretto for an operatic composition on 20 May 1919 – then Brecht's definitive rejection of Expressionism and his commitment to an unromantic realism must date from the autumn of 1917.

6

Classes with Kutscher   Conscription

It was probably towards the end of the winter term of
1917/18 that Brecht gave his paper about Johst's novel *Der Anfang*
(*The Beginning*) in a seminar led by Professor Kutscher.[1] It caused
a fearful hue and cry. Brecht rallied all his caustic wit against this
early work by the Expressionist Johst, who was later to dedicate a
play about Schlageter to Hitler, and then to become President of
both the National Socialist Writers' Academy and the Reichs-
schrifttumskammer ('Reich Chamber of Literature').[2] The recollection of this 'appalling and indefensible' paper incensed Kutscher to the end of his days; it was an essay 'bolstered with
perverse attitudes and adolescent vitriol', the like of which he had
never heard before. Indeed, despite all the criticism he himself
later suffered under the Hitler regime, he could never forgive
Brecht for this offensive attack on his star pupil. When Brecht
showed him his own play, *Baal*, in July 1918, the Professor of
Theatre took his revenge. Brecht, in his turn, said Kutscher's
criticism 'made him sick'. Even their shared admiration for
Wedekind offered no basis for reconciliation, no more than the
numerous letters which Kutscher claims to have received. As for
the disparaging remarks which Schumacher claims Artur Kutscher made about Brecht in his lectures[3] – albeit during the Third
Reich and therefore perhaps under some duress – Brecht
countered them with the laconic contention that he had never
paid any of Kutscher's tuition fees. This is a fabrication of course:
I well remember going in to pay the fees on his behalf in 1919,
and getting involved in a little contretemps with the bursary on
the very subject of how they had calculated Kutscher's dues. I

1. See pp. 158–9.
2. Leo Schlageter was a nationalist activist killed by the French during
their occupation of the Ruhr in 1923.
3. See p. 160.

myself attended one of Brecht's papers for the Kutscher seminar
in the spring of 1919; it was about Reinhard Goering's *Seeschlacht*
(*Battle at Sea*), which had had its première in the Kammerspiele
on 28 September the previous autumn. To the delight of all his
fellow students, Brecht, who had provided the play with his own
subtitle – 'or, The Convert Mutineer' – set about tearing it apart
quite ruthlessly. Only Kutscher, whose face grew darker and
more thunderous with Brecht's every word, observed with deadly
earnest that this paper only served to confirm his suspicions:
namely that Brecht was a talentless wretch.

Apart from this the summer of 1918 was long, hot and rather
dull. As a favour to Brecht, Otto Bezold engaged in a spot of illicit
breaking-and-entering in a charnel house at home in Franconia,
and purloined a couple of skulls, the finest of which has been
mentioned in all the biographies of Brecht and has achieved a
fame undreamt of while its owner was alive. Without more ado
Brecht had himself photographed with both of them, and the
pictures show him with a broad grin on his face and a death's head
tucked under each arm. He showed his gratitude to Bez later that
September with the 'Ballad of the death's head', which catalogues
the attitudes of his friends to Brecht's new acquisition.

> Heilgei says you're just an ageing fossil,
> but then Heilgei isn't too polite.
> Orge says it takes no mental muscle,
> he'd guessed your provenance all right.
>
> It's a female, look! he cried and pointed,
> Note the lack of teeth here, if you will,
> but these jaws are almost double-jointed!
> Why, this creature never had her fill!

And then they all take a turn at guessing: the skull puts Teddy in
mind of a 'sea captain', 'who drowned in cheap absinthe', Cas
Neher puts his money on 'an innocent girl',

> of the sort that put up quite a struggle,
> while she suffered transports of delight.

Brecht himself declares it to be a 'poet',

> one whose song poured sweetly forth – like cream,
> and who, bathing in a heavenly aura,
> shot a lantern in his drunken dream,

And he concludes:

> Whatsoever was your fate, it's over:
> Now you're just a warning to us all.

That he should have seen it as a warning symbol was quite appropriate given the situation: the danger of conscription was now imminent – even for registered medical students. Otto Müller had already gone; we had said our farewells to Brecht's younger brother, Walter, on the platform of the freight depot as his company left for the front; Brecht knew that it could be his turn come the autumn. Two surviving documents reveal how much it was on his mind. The first was a letter of 1918 which I received in the Bavarian forest where I happened to have met some friends of Artur Kutscher.

> Dear Herr Münsterer,
>
> Many thanks for the letter! Here we've just had the Plärrer. I've worn myself out on the swing-boats. How can anyone work much when the summer is so damn beautiful? What are you doing? I'm eating ice-cream, playing the guitar, awaiting my death sentence, and swinging at the Plärrer. And working now and then on a new play for the theatre of the future, entitled: *The Fat Man on the Swing-boat*.
>
> Please write to me about Corpse-Kutscher![4] He wrote me something about *Baal* . . .   (*Letters*, p. 55)

The second document is a visiting card he sent when he returned some books I had lent him, with a message scrawled in pencil on the back:

4. Brecht calls him 'Leichen-Kutscher': 'Leiche' (corpse), 'Kutscher' (coachman), 'Leichenkutscher' (hearse driver).

I hereby set my wordly goods in order and return these books
with thanks. All things are transient.

By the time we started our next term at school, Brecht was
already a soldier.[5]

Even at the end of 1918, when the political and military
situation was in total confusion, new recruits were still strictly
confined to barracks in the first few weeks, with the result that
Brecht's friends had no opportunity to see him. It was not until
the end of November, two weeks after the beginning of the
revolution, that I was allowed to visit him in the medical unit
where he was serving as an orderly. There have been some ghastly
accounts of the conditions under which he worked: The captain
says, 'Brecht, off with his leg!', and Brecht starts sawing away,
arms and legs flying off in all directions from the operating table.
The captain says, 'Brecht, start trepanning!' and even as he
speaks Brecht sets to with his drill, opens up the skull and pokes
about inside.[6] In fact things in Ward D of the Augsburg Reserve
Medical Station were not as bad as all that. In the fenced yard of
the local primary school at Kappeneck, not far from the Jakober
gate, they had put up primitive wooden barracks which served as
wards. The only wounds treated here were 'gentlemen's com-
plaints'. In the last throes of the war the soldiers were weary of
fighting and often resorted to this kind of 'injury', a ticket home
which could be purchased safely behind the lines from a much
sought-after breed of sales-lady.

When I visited Brecht, his superior officer was sitting hud-
dled over a microscope examining slides prepared by Gram's
method or by dark-ground illumination. Naturally he wanted to
show off the *gonococcus* and the *spirochaete bacteria* – at which
point it became abundantly clear that Brecht had no more idea
than I did what it was all about. To make up for his lack of
knowledge he had composed a song to cheer up his patients,
'Song for the gentlemen-soldiers of Ward D', and he picked up
his guitar and gave me a rendition there and then. It had, after all,

5. See pp. 140–2.
6. This is the version which originates with Sergei Tretyakov, see
Bibliography.

not been that long ago that Brecht had concocted the following lament:

> I cannot tell you the distress
> I suffer, when I see a lass
> with a yellow, silky dress
> tight across her swaying ass.

And so it was no great feat to summon up some sympathy for the poor innocent lambs, defenceless victims of love, at the mercy of every passing temptation – who simply could not restrain themselves when a taut behind swayed into view.

> How your loins did burn with fires of passion
> in your youth, when you were full of flame.
> Wenches are for loving and for thrashing,
> that's the way – man's always been the same.

The poem was very witty; and each of the three or four verses ended with the refrain:

> These womenfolk! Holy Virgin, Mother of God!
> An aching heart is bad, but worse is an aching rod!

He sang the beginning of each line slowly, charged with emotion, before rattling glibly through the rest at an unbelievable pace.

Brecht's military service was generally unexciting but even here in Augsburg an epidemic of influenza led to some upsetting confrontations with death. In consequence, Brecht's claim that he was made responsible for disposing of the bodies seems perfectly plausible.

Brecht always maintained that he was appointed to the office of soldiers' council. It has generally been assumed that he was referring to the time of the Bavarian Soviet Republic, and since his claims could not be corroborated their validity has often been doubted. It was not something that we ever talked about; however I believe that he did indeed hold such a post, even if it was only for a few days in 1918. At the very beginning of the revolution the soldiers' delegates back home were often little more than go-betweens, proposed by the officers themselves. It was their job to represent the men if they had any grievance about rations or day-to-day business, although in reality they were generally called on only if the officers wanted to ease the passage of some unpopular measure. They had no political clout. So the things Brecht later said about the insignificant nature of his office are entirely in keeping with the circumstances.

In other ways the young medical orderly did not conduct himself in a very orderly manner at all. His superiors had such a soft spot for him that they forgave him almost everything and treated him more like a sort of junior officer. Only once did he get a bit of a ticking off: when the young gentleman was allowed once more to spend his nights in the bosom of his family, he apparently deemed it quite unnecessary to appear in person at the morning roll call, and sent the kitchen-maid to report to the duty officer in his stead. On the whole though, the army did its best by Brecht, and the very best of it was that his stint came to an end after just four months. For Brecht, who hated the very thought of being pinned down, the military collective posed a considerable threat. Now there was nothing holding him back, the path to freedom was clear, life could begin.

Drums   A Second *Baal*

The first few weeks of 1919 were dominated by the events of the revolution.[1] People were burning handbills in the streets of Augsburg; on 10 January a band of mutinous sailors was formed; the name 'Spartacus' was on everybody's lips. Of course we too were caught up in the unrest. On 16 January Brecht called by. In the evening we met up again and went to the election meetings of all the different parties. We ended up late at night listening to Fechenbach, Kurt Eisner's secretary. These occasions were far from civilized; people scrambled for the front seats in the boxes and the galleries so they could shower spittle on the bald pates of the speakers. Twenty-four hours later the news leaked out that Karl Liebknecht and Rosa Luxemburg had been murdered in Berlin. On 19 January the Brecht clique got together for a shindig at Gabler's tavern. In those days our hearts were filled with revolutionary fervour – granted, we were inspired more by youthful bravado than political conviction – and yet in the midst of this almost perpetual excitement Brecht's first major collection of poems was born. It was to be called *Klampfenfibel* (*Guitar Primer*), and Cas Neher spent weeks creating water-colour illustrations aglow with colour: a guitar-playing Baal, Orge under a tree with his rope, gruesome dead soldiers on parade with bustling crowds and flags splattered against a blue spring sky, and violet shipwrecks. Brecht himself sprang new poems on us almost every day, some of which he took up into the new collection, some of which were rejected outright. On 26 January the two Brecht brothers sang Wedekind songs, and then Brecht recited some of his own poems for me. There was one about the ship's boy who tells of his travels 'from Hamburg to Pernambuco' and after each verse turns to his audience with a shrill 'Won't you come too, Sir?'; the poem tells of the poet Li T'ai-po:

1. See pp. 143–50 for more accounts of these events.

> In seventy tongues Litaipee knows what to say.
> Seventy fiends of hell are unable to seduce him.
> In seventy tongues Litaipee know how to pray.
> There are seventy tongues Litaipee can traduce in.

Yet another poem started like an old folksong:

> Once there was a youthful nun
> in the Star of Holy Mary . . .

This was an old convent in Augsburg, down below the town hall. There were some very revolutionary songs amongst them too; the 'Legend of the dead soldier' still had that splendid strophe which was repeated at the end of the poem with the lines in a different order:

> Every profession has its place.
> Musicians drum us off to war.
> The priest just pulls a pious face.
> The doctors make us fit for more.

Along with this Brecht often used to sing the 'Song of the soldiers of the red army', a dark vision reminiscent of Kollwitz, of a world caught in a struggle between hope and despair. This was much more powerful than the later version which must date from June 1919 and which appeared in the *Domestic Breviary*:

> Then, spewed by absinthe and by rot
> under the filth of city skies,
> wasted by the syphilis he'd got
> between the Holy Sisters' wide white thighs.

This anarchic song has nothing to do with the regular army of the Soviet Union; but it was obviously the danger of such a misunderstanding which later induced Brecht to suppress it despite its importance. Unless my memory fails me, 'The ship' and 'Remembering Marie A.', possibly Brecht's most famous poem, also date from this same period.

On 27 January there was a protest meeting at which Brehm's

wife[2] was invited to speak, and stirring verses were recited in honour of Rosa Luxemburg. Brecht saw the situation in a more sober, and less optimistic light. His 'Ballad of Red Rosa' was probably written soon after these events; it starts with the bitter recognition,

The red flags of the Revolutions
have long ago been swept from the roofs.

Rosa herself floats down the river, the only one 'to find freedom' in this fruitless conflict.

On 29 January we went to Ibsen's *The Lady from the Sea* in Augsburg, and soon afterwards to Wedekind's *Tod und Teufel* (*Death and the Devil*) in Munich. On 21 February Kurt Eisner was murdered, and in due course a second wave of revolution led to the short-lived Bavarian Soviet Republic. Public opinion was split – on the one side impotent rage, on the other ecstatic rejoicing: 'Shooting was too good for him,' said some, 'they should have clubbed him to death, the dirty Jew'; and when the Abbot of St Stephan's pointed out that murder was a sin, he was nearly lynched. While we in Augsburg joined the nightly rioting, stormed the courts, seized weapons from the artillery depot, and carried off our dead and wounded on stretchers improvised from fire-screens, Brecht was a spectator of events in Munich.[3] There he was comfortably installed in an eminently respectable ground-floor room, with plush furniture and photographs of 'dear departed Laura Meier' in her bridal finery, and of her late husband amongst his army chums. These were just the right surroundings for Brecht's new play, *Spartacus*, which he dashed off in three days. He wrote it as a money-spinner and thought it artistically vastly inferior to *Baal*.

On 24 February and for the next few days I met up with Brecht in Munich. I was about to be expelled from school for political reasons, and I also had a family tragedy to contend with.[4]

2. Lilli Prem (see pp. 147–9).   3. See pp. 145–6.
4. See p. 158 for the threat of expulsion. The Münsterer family, like many German officers' families, found themselves in financial diffi-culties after the war. Hanns Otto's father was unemployed and it seemed unlikely that the son would be able to go to university.

We discussed these problems, but above all we talked about the play and its prospects. In March it was presented to Lion Feuchtwanger, who was a sort of writer in residence at the Kammerspiele in Augustenstraße and had enormous influence. At the beginning of April Brecht seemed very hopeful: things were starting to move. Feuchtwanger was so taken with the young playwright and his hero Thomas Kragler that he sat down to write a play of his own. It was announced for the 1919/20 season as *Thomas Brecht*, but when it appeared as a book the title had been changed to *Thomas Wendt*. It was Feuchtwanger's first attempt at a literary portrait of Brecht, and a total failure it was too; Kaspar Pröckl in the novel *Success* is something of an improvement.[5] We were not at all impressed by the whole business, but in the event there is so little similarity between the two plays that it was almost enough for Brecht to re-christen his Thomas as Andreas Kragler. Now there was no more talk of staging the play, despite its topicality, and the manuscript of *Drums in the Night*, as it was now called, sat yellowing in Feuchtwanger's desk. And there it stayed until 1921 when it came to the notice of Rudolf Frank.[6] The play which Brecht had written only for the box office, and in which he had long since lost interest, was suddenly hailed as the best 'coming-home' play of the war. It was for this, together with *Baal* and *In the Jungle of Cities*, that Brecht was awarded the Kleist Prize. Later of course Brecht deplored the despicable behaviour of his hero,[7] who abandons his comrades on the barricades and slips off to bed with his second-hand bride. There are no banners, no filmic panegyrics to the victory of the proletariat as in *The Mother*; the renegade hurls his drum at the moon, which turns out to be nothing more than a paper lantern, and the play ends on a tender love-scene: 'Are you warm enough?' – 'It's been four whole years . . .' It is true that this is the shabbiest of all possible solutions, but at least it is the most vital.

Vitality was our great rallying cry. By 10 March Brecht had

5. For more on Feuchtwanger's impressions of Brecht, see pp. 163–4.
6. See p. 164.
7. Münsterer is referring here to Brecht's later autocritique, 'On looking through my first plays' (see *Collected Plays*, pp. 437–9).

already written bits of yet another play, *Absalom*, and in April he returned to *Baal* with renewed vigour. We idled away our days in Gabler's tavern and Zanantoni's ice-cream parlour – where Brecht exchanged small-talk with 'la patrona' or got out his guitar, danced with the pretty waitress and spun her a line about the imminent communization of women; and yet in the midst of this we burned with a feverish and chaotic creativity, almost as if our lives depended on it.

> If all you do is shit, says Baal, I say,
> that's still worth more than doing sweet f.a.

That seems to have been the guiding principle of our way of life. A couple of minor events had consequences. On 18 March old Ernst Possart held a poetry reading in the Ludwigsbau.[8] By now he cut a pretty senile figure, peering at his programme: 'The God and the dancing girl' . . . After a long theatrical pause he threw back his head and started: 'Mahadöh, Lord of all', he read, and continued, with exaggerated pathos, right the way through to 'up to heaven'. Then the subtitle caught his eye: 'Indian Legend', and, after the customary pause for effect, off he went again, head thrown back, voice brimming with emotion: 'Mahadöh, Lord of all'. It was awful. Brecht, of course, did a marvellous imitation; his 'Possart-Mahadöh' was a *pièce de résistance*, and subsequently he decided to arrange Goethe's ballad for guitar. On 14 April the first public reading of Brecht's own poems took place, at a memorial service for the fallen of the Augsburg sports club. Brecht had composed a prologue and epilogue for it, but was unable to resist suggesting that there be a similar service for the 'fallen women' of the club. In the gloomy hall, lit by just two flickering torches, 'Frl. Vera-Maria Eberle, of Augsburg city theatre' recited the two poems from an impressive folder. As I remember, the first depicted the cheering troops, heads held high, marching off to war, and the second the tragic outcome. 'Our heroes lie slaughtered before us' was Brecht's grim conclusion, and there was no mention of 'dulce et decorum', nor of rising up to march again in spirit. Even then we were not much

8. See also pp. 124–5.

enamoured of Eberle's rendition, and subsequently Brecht landed himself with a libel action on account of some criticisms to which the actress took particular exception.[9]

The most important event of that spring was the revision of *Baal*.[10] On 2 May, the same day as the downfall of the Bavarian Soviet Republic, Brecht read us the new version, with the cannon fire in Munich rumbling faintly in the distance. Whole sections of the first part of the play had been cut, in particular the scenes in the newspaper office in which Baal clings to the notion of some kind of ordered lifestyle. So it all appeared even less civilized and even less bourgeois. Over the next few days there were even more changes. To counter the charge of brutish chauvinism a scene of relative forbearance was introduced. On 4 May the whole episode of Johannes and the forgotten umbrella was cut, along with the rape of Sophie Dechant (Sophie Barger in the later printed version), and the splendid first scenes on the open country road. The earlier 'Hotel Continental' scene had been replaced by a scene in the drivers' inn, and so Baal sings a rather cruder song than before. There was a new character too, in the person of a shady nigger-businessman who was very soon to be taken out again, a precursor of the character called Mjurk. On 6 May Brecht read us the brand-new scene about the cattle, which we discussed in depth. One of the last additions, as far as I can remember, was the scene with the tramp, which develops the idea of the Corpus Christi procession of *Urbaal*. Every day the text was further changed and rearranged: the three seduction scenes were condensed and linked by the interludes with the beggar's organ, and as the finishing touch Brecht even thought up the cynical motto, 'Cacatum est. Stop. Non pictum.' By 20 May Brecht was sufficiently happy with his manuscript to give it to me to read through, and willingly accepted a few of my suggested alterations. There was to be a reading to test audience reaction to the wild succession of scenes, but it came to grief on account of Brecht's

9. See pp. 160-2.

10. The history of *Baal* has been explored by Dieter Schmidt (see Bibliography). The most recent accounts diverge in some respects from Münsterer's.

bashfulness. Time and again we rounded up our acquaintances in a café, where Brecht had promised to read, and each time it was the same old story: we waited for hours, and then skulked off with our tails between our legs, having seen neither hide nor hair of either Brecht or Baal.

Baal left his imprint on our lives, however; that early summer of 1919 was imbued with the spirit of the play. But the reverse was also true; Brecht's play, especially in this second and most successful draft, was filled with impressions of our own lives. Of course it is not any sort of *roman à clef*, but it is shot through with the colours and textures of Augsburg: Brecht's garret in Bleichstraße and his table laden with papers, the nut bushes along the banks of the Lech, the birch saplings adorning the walls for Corpus Christi, and the dingy taverns by the town moat and in Hettenbach. Even some of the characters have recognizable traits, and in some of the dialogues there is no great gulf between fiction and fact. The same songs that were bawled out in the shabby dives and liquor-dens of *Baal* were sung by Brecht and his friends in their night-time revels in Gabler's tavern: 'Ballad of the adventurers', 'loping through hells and flogged through paradises', or the lullaby:

> The earth may be spinning, the skies too perhaps,
> Who gives a damn, if you're pickled in schnapps,

with its heartless lines,

> Floating downstream with rats in your hair,
> the sky's still above you, wondrous fair.

The Wolfszahn, a meadow between the Lech and Wertach, with tall trees, lush grass and dipping willows, where we used to go to swim and laze about in the sun, was the setting for just the same 'wonderful tales' with which Baal leads youths and maids alike 'to his trough'. And in those days, in Lechhausen, the fields of corn stretched right into the middle of town, just as in *Baal*. Of course, anywhere in the world the skies may be blue, orange or violet, and the nights clear and crisp with stars, and anywhere the young may feel their pulses quicken, but we were young in Augsburg then.

For me every street corner of the old town holds some memory of Brecht. Brecht used to meet me out of school by the Hundestein next to St Stephan's. Beneath the city ramparts on the edge of the Jakober suburb there was a modest little inn with a type of orchestrion: when you put ten pfennigs in, a sentimental melody began to play, a painted scene lit up, and a foaming waterfall appeared with clouds creaking slowly back and forth. It made a big impression on Brecht. It was, as he himself admitted, an inspiration for the poem 'The heaven for disenchanted men' – and doubtless also for the music to his plays, which is characterized by that same strange mechanical sound and the omission of some notes, like a musical box with some of the teeth missing. Down by the town moat, not far from the 'House of the Seven Children', which took its name from the relief on the Roman sarcophagus in the wall, was a bench, surrounded by chestnut trees.[11] There we sat on the evening of 29 May; perhaps it was raining, the branches were dripping overhead. Brecht had just been berating me and had reproached me with my middle-class respectability. It was lucky that it was dark, so that no one could see how small and pathetic I felt. Suddenly he turned to me: 'Incidentally, shouldn't we call each other "du"?' I only remember how long I clasped his hand in mine, knowing that now I truly belonged to that happy band of outcasts.[12]

And then there were all the different pubs where we would down a few beers or a cheap schnapps. Our favourite was Gabler's, where there was a long narrow snug off the main bar, fitted out with painted wooden furniture. There were two stuffed eels in a glass case, one had lost its head, and a swordfish (or was it a crocodile?) hung from the ceiling. That was the setting for all the big Brecht get-togethers.

11. When Brecht was a baby the family lived briefly in a block called 'Bei den sieben Kindeln'. In fact the relief is a warning and depicts only six children at play: the seventh was said to have drowned in the River Lech which rushes past the house.

12. The band called themselves the 'Verworfenen' (outcasts, reprobates).

Amongst my most precious memories are those night-time processions through the streets of the old town, Brunnlech, Graben, Pfannenstiel and Lueginsland. Brecht would strum the broken strings of his guitar, and sing 'The heaven for disenchanted men':

Midway between the dusking and the dawn,
naked and freezing in a rock-strewn glen,
among the heavens, concealed, forlorn,
must be the heaven for disenchanted men.

Or he improvised a cantata, perhaps even an opera about the beauties of the May evening, and Orge played the maestro, gesticulating wildly and whipping an imaginary orchestra to a frenzied furioso. Often we would clamber over the barbed-wire fences of the city walls and offer up serenades to the belles of Augsburg, or we would just sit dangling our legs over the edge, Brecht with his guitar, another friend with his fiddle, a third holding a lantern on a rod. Sometimes we even had a sizeable audience, and as we marched through the streets 'admirers' young and old flocked behind us. We would sometimes sing the old folksong about the Bavarian hussar:

A brave hussar did once adore
his sweetheart a full year or more . . .

Now I have worn my coloured dress,
now I must wear my mourning dress,
for this and countless lonely years.
My grief will live through all my years.

Or we might sing Goethe's 'Rat-catcher', a few Wedekind songs or anything by Brecht himself which seemed to fit the occasion. For example 'The old man in spring', who finds no cause for envy, since:

. . . in my early you-outh
the spring was surely that much fairer then.
But pretty girls were fairer too, forsoo-ooth,
and that remains a comfort for old men.

There were several real gems amongst them, like the ˙'Bitter love-song':

> However that may be,
> there was a time I loved her . . .
>
> All of the girls, I've long since forgotten them,
> yet I remember they were good to kiss then,
> only of her, my most truly belov'd, I know
> not even this.

Some evenings we were down by the river. My diary for 22 May reports:

> Evening on the banks of the Lech. We sat on the ground, Bert, Otto Müller and I. The sky high, wide and wonderfully blue, fading to orange and finally to violet. Beneath us the crystal, foaming river, and in the distance the black silhouette of the town with its towers and rooftops. The grass was damp with dew. Brecht was singing.

Five days later we were leaning on the bridge over the Lech:

> The banks are lost in a haze of blue. It seems to me, this must be a foreign vessel and we are standing in the bows, gazing down into the yellow Ganges, yellow with loam from the melting snows of the Himalayas, and we are adrift in a distant Indian night. Bert was writing.

Brecht honestly did need to capture his ideas as we walked, for there was such a torrent of dramatic and lyric inspiration.

On hot afternoons we would go swimming in the Hahnreibach, lie naked in the Wolfszahn meadow, or go climbing trees, as Brecht describes it in one of the 'Gospels' which he read me there on 11 June.[13] On 8 June five of us were assembled there, and Brecht recited funeral orations and devotions, which began with the words 'Beloved in Christ' and seemed so grotesque that

13. 'Of climbing in trees' (*Poems*, p. 29), one of the poems which best captures this mood, from the *Domestic Breviary*.

we doubled up with laughter and rolled around in the reeds. The next day provoked philosophical musings. Brecht proclaimed that we owe our existence to the humidity of our planet, to chance, we are nothing more than purposeless creatures, clods of earth, formed of a passing fancy, and of water. And yet we can think and enjoy. To what end? Our understanding is so paltry. In the evening he read to us from Verlaine and Rilke.

Idyllic Days   Two Poems

Another of the special pleasures of our youth in Augsburg
was the Plärrer, a traditional fair held on the little parade-ground
twice a year, in early spring and late summer. There is an early
poem of Brecht's:

> The tumbling spring came a-leaping
> through the hoop of the sky to the ground
> with organs, singing and piping
> the fair was back in town.

The meadow was small; you could take it all in at a glance. To the
left of the entrance old Jonathan had a stall where he peddled his
tattered books – 'Gentlefolks only buy books with their first pages
missing' – and next to it he had a rather mangy peep-show: 'Three
days in heaven, three days on earth and three days in Hades, all
for 10 pfennigs, 15 pfennigs with a commentary!' Then came the
side-shows, a carousel with aeroplanes, the toboggan-ride, the
circus, the snake-ladies, the lions, a tightrope dancer with a fat
bottom – which always drew a big round of applause – and clowns
and big cats too. Of course we went to all the shows, the wax
cabinet and Schichtl's guillotine, but our great passion was for the
swing-boats.[1] 'The swings are all you need to save you from
bourgeois respectability,' declared Brecht, and in an early play
which he mentions in his letter of August 1918 he evidently
wanted to portray the exhilarating liberation of a poor innocent
citizen who gets caught up in the hurly-burly of a carnival and the
rhythm of the swing-boats. As for the girls, he reckoned swinging
with them was as good as sleeping with them. For us it became a
symbol of life – working your way up until the prow of the swing

---

1. August Schichtl first exhibited a guillotine at the Munich October
festival in the late nineteenth century. For the swing-boats, see
pp. 127–8.

nudged the canopy – or, if the roof was open, you were hurled out past the flickering lights into the blue night-sky where you could look down on all the glittering splendours of the world below, before that inescapable plunge back down to earth. 'Thus are the damned shown all the bliss of the blessed, before they are cast down into the darkness.' We used to go swinging with Bi, or with the girls from Steinicke's who had their evenings free and were happy to tag along. We were delighted to discover how the same fear which makes men ugly actually makes women more beautiful. Late at night we would straggle home through the sleepy streets of the old Imperial City, a motley procession. Käthe Hupfauer[2] would bawl out Shakespearian profanities – 'Hold your tongue, cur!' – in all possible variations, and Brecht would improvise splendid Wagner parodies, like the Tristanesque aria 'Come hither Ina, my beloved', which he addressed to his wolfhound.

When I look back to that May, I remember a brief romantic idyll in which Brecht also played a part. One of our schoolfriends had two charming sisters, the younger, Maruschka, exuberant and jolly, the other, Therese, quiet and nut-brown, with splendid eyes so dark they were almost black. Since I knew her brother, who wanted to become a priest, I was allowed to visit their strict Catholic household, which reminded me of Goethe's Sesenheim with its rigid patriarchal rule.[3] Of course I laughed and joked with the younger sister, but I only had eyes for the elder, whose whole being radiated simplicity and goodness. I was fascinated by the animation of her face, from her impish grin to her stern inquisitorial gaze – all set off by a sweet little moustache. In order to snatch a few moments alone with her one had to waylay her on the way home from May devotions. Every now and again one of

2. One of the girls who worked at Steinicke's bookshop. Long after Brecht had left Augsburg she ran the shop herself for a time.
3. Münsterer is referring to Goethe's Sesenheimer poems (1770–1) which were addressed to the daughter of a pastor in the Alsatian village of Sesenheim. He confuses the ages of the sisters: Maruschka was in fact the elder. For more on Brecht's 'romance' with Therese Ostheimer see pp. 130–2.

us was successful; but all too often she slipped away in the crowd, and the duped suitor was left to face the taunts of his friends. This pretty lass was Brecht's first, if unrequited, love. When he was eighteen he had once followed her home, and just caught up with her at the gate of her house. 'Excuse me, Miss, there's something I want to say to you,' he stammered. 'And I have *nothing* to say to you,' came the immediate response, and with that she disappeared into the house. All the same, as her brother told me many years later, Brecht wrote her a long and earnest letter, which was intercepted by her father. This was back in 1916, and the whole thing seemed to have blown over, but now Brecht began pressing me to arrange another meeting. A sleight of hand with some theatre tickets provided me with the opportunity to introduce her to the poet. She behaved marvellously, and in a way she was, I think, head and shoulders above us all. But, as I had foreseen, there could be no common ground for two such different souls: there was an unbridgeable gulf between Brecht, with his uninhibited and precarious attitudes, and her shuttered life of religious and familial obligations. And so it all fizzled out after one brief encounter, and one fine poem. It is the ballad about the blue ship which appears on the horizon, blue as the sea and the sky, heeded by no one, shunned by all.

> One day in spring a ship hove into sight
> From distant shores and as the ocean blue
> With flapping sails and hatches battened tight
> Unaccounted for, and not a soul for crew.
>
> It lay there rocking many sun-drenched days
> and many watched it from the sunny shore.
> It lay so long it faded in the haze
> and no one saw its blue hull any more.
>
> Only drunkards reeling through night's chill
> would hear strange music echo from the rig,
> and yet: not one of those who listened still,
> and yet: not one who saw the sails fill,
> took courage in his hands to board the brig.

It followed on a foreign star
to seek its rest on distant sands –
for, come the spring, the ghostly ship was far,
drifting to the shores of blue-hazed lands.

It bears the title 'Romanticism' and according to Brecht he composed it in a boat on the Tegernsee, where he had a job for a while
as a private tutor. In September 1917 it was presented, in a
particularly fine cover made specially for the purpose, to the
'pretty gardener' – as we called her, after her home in
Gartenstraße. This little poem proved its usefulness on several
occasions and, in the good old tradition of the troubadours and
minnesingers, other young ladies received it in their turn and
were flattered to think it had been written for them. If the truth
be told, however, it was born of this first, hesitant and unrequited
affection.

For many years I have cherished fond memories of those May
nights, the smell of incense in the cathedral and the outings on the
moat. However, there is only one little poem of my own which,
like Brecht's, has survived the ravages of time. It is called 'Stadtgraben im Frühling' ('The town-moat in spring') and the scent of
those spring days still clings to it.

Always when springtime comes, boats in the still night air
rock on the water, always when springtime comes,
girls sing, the branches drip down their dew on us,
and from the walls the blossoms come drifting.

When you were but a youth, drunk with the night of May,
wreathed round with incense, then from the minster you
walked to the town moat. Down in the half-light of
trembling torches, gondolas waited.

Shyly you leant your head, hot with the song of night,
there on the tree-trunk. Dew fell and pollen dust
covered your hands when, suddenly, lips brushed on
lips in a blissful burning sensation.

Years now have passed since then. Now your own son
                                                perhaps
stands by the chestnuts. Even a grandson might
steer the small boat out: still the trees turn to green,
still the girls' laughter rings through the darkness.

Such is the spring night-air. If you spent centuries
in the grave sleeping, till your name long ago
had been forgotten: still the song would be sung,
girls would be laughing, branches be dripping dew,
down through the endless cycle of ages.

Politics   Philosophy

In the spring and above all the summer of 1919 scarcely a day
went by without my meeting Brecht. It was a most productive
time, all sorts of projects were weighed up and discussed, and
there was nothing which did not somehow arise. One day at the
end of April I awoke bathed in tears; I had dreamt that Brecht
was dead and I was at a sort of funeral service. My subconscious
had probably confused the memory of Brecht's poems at the
memorial for the fallen that same month with my fear of losing
my friend. Naturally I raced straight to Bleichstraße and found
Bert lying in bed, bandaged head to toe and covered in bruises.
He had tried his hand at riding with Otto Müller the day before,
but it had all gone horribly wrong. His injuries turned out to be
pretty harmless; he was only grazed and set my mind immediately
at rest when he started reciting from his most recent work.

One of the subjects he found particularly interesting was
pedagogy. This was evidently a hereditary trait which he had
from his schoolteacher forebears. Although I knew nothing of
these ancestors, I always noticed, even then, how much of a
schoolteacher there was in our young revolutionary. On 19 April
for example, he outlined at length his ideas for an effective educational programme for the young. On starting school every child
would be given a number and would be addressed by this number
until it had engaged the teacher's sympathy with its ready answers
and had thereby won the right to be addressed by name. Brecht
would demonstrate the basics of morality and the necessity of
learning, using children's games such as Cowboys and Indians.
For particularly diligent or gifted children he suggested special
afternoon lessons which were not open to the others. He could, he
believed, prod habitual liars and children with other defects of
character back on to the straight-and-narrow with a mixture of
irony and scorn. As reward for outstanding achievement in the

more senior classes, Brecht's educational programme envisaged permission to visit a girl. I am sure that Brecht provided precise details of all this; unfortunately, however, there are only hints in my diaries, so I shall have to leave the elaboration to the appropriate authorities in the Ministry of Education.

Another time – I was not present myself – Brecht proposed in front of the whole group that children should be taken away from their parents, raised by the state and, at least up to a certain age, educated communally. Käthe Hupfauer, one of the three Steinicke girls, did not take kindly to this at all. She gave him a severe ticking off: how could he, who had been so mollycoddled in the bosom of his family, and who really could not complain that he was neglected or unloved, how could he talk such nonsense! This outburst was greeted with universal dismay. Everyone treated Brecht with kid gloves; and one of the group who had taken a shine to Käthe duly informed her, on one of their routine forays in Karolinenstraße, that she had ruined everything and that from now on the Brecht clique were sure to cut her dead. 'We'll soon see about that,' said the Hupfauer girl. She marched resolutely up to the approaching band and said with a winning smile, 'Gentlemen, may I invite you round for an ice-cream this afternoon?' And lo and behold, they all accepted, everybody came, there was no question of anybody cutting her. Brecht himself, or so Käthe would relate even years later, gobbled down the ice-cream straight from the serving dish.

Several of Brecht's pedagogic ideas were subsequently put to the test. Some, like the schools for gifted students, proved successful; others, in particular the excessive interventions of the state, led to disastrous abuses, which Brecht himself later portrayed and analysed in scenes of *Fear and Misery of the Third Reich*.

Of course we also talked about women and love, and about the sincere, untainted joy which Brecht said that he derived from such experiences. He repeatedly assured everyone that he could not be relied upon – that was a facet of his polygamous nature. One thing, however, that always amazed me was his unique ability to inspire everyone who came at all close to him with a philosophy of life which even made separation possible without great bitterness. These lines on love bear witness to that:[1]

You ask how long now have they been together?
But briefly.
                    And how soon they'll separate?
                                                   Time's short.
Thus love appears to lovers their support.

It is possible that Ziffel in *Refugee Conversations* is thinking of some specific events when he speaks of the minor acts of brutality which, from time to time, became unavoidable. All the same, I do not believe that there was one of Brecht's female companions for whom the time with him did not mean an immeasurable gain: they became greater in spirit and more desirable too.[2] He was marvellously gifted with a rare combination of wit and charm, which was a joy to man and woman alike. Of course one cannot deny that an encounter with genius is at once both a delight and a curse. Everything must be judged in a new light; there are bound to be sorrows. So much seems just beyond one's grasp, and in this life every ounce of joy must be accounted for. The young Brecht was convinced of that.

Politically we were remarkably naive, and none of us could be said to have had any firm political allegiance at that time. Brecht later often admitted his complete ignorance of even quite rudimentary matters. Of course we had heard of Marx, Engels, Kautsky and Lenin, but what we had heard of them was invariably at second or third hand and only really amounted to a few bits and pieces gleaned from some pamphlet or other. I had my own copies of Landauer and of Eisner's speeches for example, but that was not the way to learn much about the basics of Marxism, or about economic and social theory. It is quite possible that our instinctive opposition to the aspects of bourgeois life which encroached upon our own day-to-day existence played quite a

1. They were later included as part of a song ('The Lovers') in *Rise and Fall of the City of Mahagonny*.
2. For further views on Brecht and women see pp. 130–7 and 151–5.

large part in our developing sympathy for left-wing politics. I
remember how one day Brecht demonstrated the advantages of
the Soviet system with compelling dialectics, but concluded, all
the same, that Bolshevism was a sickness which would be overcome – although not before it had brought about our downfall.[3]
Brecht always wanted to restrain my own syndicalist leanings and
poured cold water on my wide-eyed belief in the essential equality
of people. It was not a matter of the flesh itself, but also of the
centuries of education and conditioning to which this flesh had
been subjected. This was once more the voice of the schoolmaster; and he was right, in so far as even the most resolute
democracy can do little good without a certain measure of
aristocracy.

Moreover, our sympathies were wide-ranging. When Otto
Bezold stood up to speak at a Communist meeting and pointed
out the responsibilities of the factory owners and the risks which
they incur – the well-being of the workers is dependent on them –
we applauded him for the courage of his convictions. Not one of
the supporters of the bourgeois parties would have dared to speak
up like that. Only Otto Müller went so far as to fight on the side of
the anti-republican forces and get a job spying for Epp[4] in
Munich, and he had to put up with some good-natured teasing. In
the event he soon left the Freikorps. He and other eye-witnesses
described to us the horrors of the collapse of the Munich Soviet.
While under arrest Gustav Landauer was trampled to death by
soldiers' boots; the corpses of the men, women and children who
had been shot in the slaughter-house were heaped on carts and
rattled through the streets so that their battered skulls smashed
against the cobblestones and their brains spilt out into the gutter;
we ourselves were witness to a procession of prisoners on the way
to execution in the gravel-pit – they were spat upon and splattered
with excrement by the lackeys of officialdom who had crept out of
their hiding-places to enjoy the spectacle. Such images cannot
ever be forgotten. Brecht must have had these scenes before his

3. See p. 146.
4. Franz Ritter von Epp, Freikorps leader who helped to crush the
Munich Soviet in 1919. See also p. 148.

eyes when, many years later, in the notes to *The Tutor*[5] he spoke of the essential barbarity of the counter-revolution.

Time and again, throughout our youth, it was impressed upon us that man, as *zoön politikon*, is at the mercy of politics. So it comes as no surprise that Brecht, in a conversation on 18 May, attempted to demonstrate the divinity of Christ by reference to nothing other than his total rejection of the political. Pilate's question, 'Are you the Son of God?' was based, as Brecht saw it, on an inappropriate Roman preconception and was thus greeted simply with the answer, 'You say that I am.' The great teacher did not even attempt to resolve the misunderstanding. It was only after the resurrection that he made everything clear. In his youth Brecht never rejected the essentials of Christian doctrine; his criticisms were directed rather against what he considered to be a falsification – a falsification moreover which significantly derived from that favourite apostle of the Lutheran church, St Paul. This may be one of the reasons why he showed greater sympathy for Catholicism than for the confession of his own upbringing. Of course he also could not abide the puritanical pride and cant which flourish so abundantly in this part of Germany. Strangely enough, Catholicism was the religion of his father; his mother, who had far more sympathy for the young poet, was a Protestant.

Brecht's relationship with philosophy in this early period was just as inconsistent as his attitude to religion. His understanding of philosophy was not one of an uncompromising quest for truth, but more of a careful process of negotiation with the immutable facts of existence, something half-way between western worldly wisdom and oriental sagacity, which might best be described as a 'catechism of life'. Where it was a matter of pure intellect and logical deduction he was often surpassed by his friends. Nevertheless, he always stuck to his guns and defended his point of view with some fairly dubious arguments – until the very next day, when he would expound our own opinions, as if they stood to reason and he had never doubted them.

In those days we were still close to the natural world too,

5. Brecht's adaptation (in 1949–50) of J. M. R. Lenz's *Der Hofmeister*.

although later Brecht was to fall under the spell of the metropolis and distance himself from all that. We used to wander through forest and meadow, drinking in the natural beauty; in the early poems, trees, rivers and starlit nights abound in almost romantic profusion. Sometimes it seemed as if Brecht was a little ashamed of these feelings. When I once showed him my collection of flowering cactuses, he was very taken with them. He was particularly impressed that such prickly, leather-skinned plants could proffer those huge velvety blossoms, all the while protesting their innocence, as if they had nothing at all to do with it. He did not develop these ideas, but perhaps he was thinking of the tender beauty of some of his own poems and his pretence of imperturbable indifference.

Summer Symphony   Poetry and Prose

It is one of the many paradoxes of Brecht's life that our summer of compulsive sloth in 1919 was at the same time a period of feverish creativity. Brecht had time in abundance, but he demanded an abundance of time from others too. When a young lady, whom we invited to go boating, declined saying she was too busy, Brecht flew off the handle. On her own head be it, he stormed, 'I can't stand people who always have work to do; they're like those idiots who are for ever washing their hands, for fear of a bit of muck; work is simply compound idleness.' In fact, the reverse might have been more accurate, for these months of indolence proved to be some of the most creative and fruitful of Brecht's entire life. As I said before, the brief note in my diary that night on the Lech sums it up: 'Bert was writing.' Bert was always writing. Everyone who knew him must have been amazed at his constant stream of ideas and plans, and at the apparent effortlessness of his writing. In fact it cost him a lot of effort, as he himself admitted many years later. The numerous drafts and versions bear witness to that. Jack London's autobiographical novel, *Martin Eden*, relates how painstaking the apprenticeship of the writer can be. Despite his youthful rejection of intellectualism, Brecht was meticulous in the learning of his craft; and he demanded of us, for example, that we should be able to keep up an off-the-cuff debate in perfect hexameters.

I have already discussed the progress of *Baal* that spring. By the end of May Brecht had already completed the greater part of a tragedy called *Condel*, which, as I remember, owed much to Büchner. In June he was working on a comedy – 'in collaboration', so he said, with Jakob Geis,[1] but Brecht was doubtless

---

1. A Munich dramaturg with an important influence at the Nationaltheater.

firmly in control. This was supposed to be a money-spinner and was full of concessions to popular taste. I believe the working title was *Herr Meier and His Son*, but Brecht never read me anything from it. On 22 July the scenario to *Herr Makrot* was sketched out in my little summer-house in Pasing.

One might regret that Brecht later abandoned these projects, but the many completed works are surely adequate recompense. The fate of two other larger theatrical projects is quite a different matter: Brecht worked on them for most of the year, and one of them had reached an advanced state of completion by December 1919. The first originally bore the title *David* (or *Absalom?*), *or God's Chosen One*. Later it was changed to *Absalom and Bathsheba*.[2] The story is taken from the Bible. Although in the play Absalom is the most sympathetic character, it is David who is 'God's favourite' – despite the immorality which is apparent even in the Scriptures. The opening scene shows Absalom in the court-yard listening to the guards' salacious anecdotes about the escapades of the ageing king. Suddenly the lowering silhouette of David appears above the battlements: 'I call my son Absalom to account!' The curtain falls on ominous silence. It is an exposition Brecht might have been proud of even in his maturity. Amongst the high points were Absalom's conversation with the trees, and a tender love-scene when Bathsheba escapes from David and flees to her beloved Absalom in the field. The structure of the play was enormously involved, because of the central importance given to the lovers' relationship and David's cunning ruses to implicate Uriah in Bathsheba's pregnancy. To this day I do not know how he solved this particular problem. What I do know is that even years later I was convinced that this play, had it been completed, would have numbered amongst the greatest works of all German drama.

The structure of *Summer Symphony* was even more compli-cated. One draft overlayed another in a constant process of revision and correction. By the end of the year, the work was almost finished. Its centrepiece was the story of the widow of

2. In December 1920 Brecht included a brief recommendation of André Gide's *Bathsheba* in a review for the *Volkswille* (GW, vol. 15, p. 35).

Ephesus, from Petronius.[3] She has decided to starve herself to death in her dead husband's vault when one of the guards comes over to comfort her. Then, when the corpse of a condemned man is stolen she allows the body of her husband to be hung up in its place. Brecht, however, transposed the whole episode to a setting in Germany in an indeterminate past sometime before the Reformation or at the time of the Peasants' War. A troupe of actors brings life, and consternation, into the petit-bourgeois world, by singing wicked songs to incite the people to libidinous acts – 'Over the tops of the trees the devil's abroad'. In a pasture at dusk a forerunner of Paul Ackermann (in *Mahagonny*) sings 'Lucifer's evening song', which later appears, as the chorale 'Against temptation', in both the *Domestic Breviary* and the opera *Mahagonny*. There are indeed many close correspondences with *Mahagonny*; the setting may be completely different, but in the theme – an explosive rejection of order in the face of extreme peril – there are undeniable similarities. Of course, *Summer Symphony* could never have been performed: each individual scene would have been enough to provoke a glorious scandal – like those occasioned by such comparatively harmless plays as Wedekind's *Schloß Wetterstein* or even Lautensack's *Gelübde* (*The Vow*). Brecht did not dare dictate the text to a secretary. Even for the first version of *Baal* he had found a friend to perform this delicate task for him. The outrageous *Summer Symphony* never progressed beyond a rough manuscript, and perhaps that is why.

Four or five of Brecht's one-act plays have survived from that autumn of 1919: *The Dead Dog* is a dialogue between a king and a beggar bewailing the death of his dog; *The Wedding* is the only one of these plays that was later performed, and even in Frankfurt it met with the customary storms of protest. Then there were the rustic farce *Driving Out a Devil* and *Lux in Tenebris*. In the latter Brecht treats the theme of bourgeois capitalism for the first time, describing the competition between two business enterprises which eventually join forces, namely the Brothel and the Moral Mission. The last of the plays, *The Catch*, was not included in the

3. Petronius is thought to be the author of the satirical picaresque Latin novel, known as the *Satyricon*, from which this story comes.

typescript which Brecht gave me to look over on 28 November 1919. At the time I was not impressed by *The Dead Dog*; dramatically it was the weakest of the plays but its language was very powerful. Looking back, these scenes seem reminiscent of Karl Valentin, whom Brecht so much admired, but they have something of Courteline too, and perhaps even anticipate Ionesco. Brecht himself acknowledged the bawdy interludes by Cervantes as his primary model.

This impressive dramatic output was accompanied by a veritable flood of lyric poems. Some of these are amongst the pearls of the *Domestic Breviary*, but many equally valuable poems were lost; some of course were simply inferior and were rightly rejected. Brecht's opinion of so-called 'literary achievement' is well known, and his own work was never intended to be pure, unadulterated gold, but rather an ore, shot through with individual, precious veins. Some poems can be dated approximately from the diaries, or at least they can be assigned a latest date. On 19 April Brecht sang me a ballad about a laundry-man with the refrain:

> And he waded through the mess, mess, mess,
> but the mess, it grew no less.

This was undoubtedly one of the weakest of Brecht's poems, yet its obvious counterpart, 'Song of the ruined innocent folding linen', was considered worthy of inclusion in *Hundert Gedichte (One Hundred Poems)* over thirty years later.[4] On 18 May I heard, probably for the first time, the 'Song of the Mother Army':

> This night there was a battle
> and the foe was there, oh mama.

On 16 June I heard the 'The soldier of the red army' and on 2 December the 'Ballad of the dear Lord'. This poem was accompanied by a drawing which portrays a man in a long robe peering inquisitorially in through the window at a little child in

---

4. *Hundert Gedichte 1918–1950*, edited by Wieland Herzfelde, Berlin (East), 1952, was the first German-language post-war anthology of Brecht's poetry.

bed with tousled hair. The drawing suggests that this is the poem which later became familiar as 'Report on a tick' and which sends up the pietist attitude to God. All of these were performed by Brecht to guitar accompaniment. For 5 August my notes record that he sang the 'Ballad of the negro'. Probably this was the song of the 'fortunate woman' who lacks nothing and yet dreams of a negro:

> She was blest with fortune and pleasure
> like the laughing blue of the sky,
> her joys were beyond all measure:
> the apple of any man's eye.

For a while we had quite a fad for negroes. In *Drums in the Night* Balicke demands, 'Is she waiting for the Pope? Or does it have to be a nigger?', and a 'nigger-scene' was added to *Baal*, from which Brecht was always singing:

> This young negro was not grand,
> nor was he good-looking,
> nor was he refined, it's true,
> but he was well known to the boys in blue.

In Brecht's ironic 'Political reflections by the lake' there is another mention of negroes. The voice is probably that of an Augsburg grammar-school teacher who is dismayed to see the young folks having fun in spite of the 'black affront', as the participation of black French soldiers in the occupation of the Rhineland was known. He underlines the threat by observing that the Babylonians also 'went boating' on the eve of disaster. Amongst Brecht's plans for this period there was even a 'negro play', a sort of black equivalent of Wedekind's hero, the Marquis von Keith, who reaches the highest echelons of society but then, in a rush of frenzied nostalgia for his 'jungle origins', destroys every last vestige of social respectability by dancing naked through the theatre.

As far as I remember Brecht also had the idea of publishing a separate little book of more intimate poems alongside the *Domestic Breviary* during that summer of 1919. They were to be called *My Achilles Poems*.[5] Later, in deference to Aretino and with the place of publication in mind, they became the *Augsburg Sonnets*, although they make frequent reference to Berlin life and are by no means all sonnets. The publication of this collection was interrupted in 1927, after the type had been set up for only the first page. The manuscript was lost and it seems impossible to reconstruct the contents of the work with any degree of certainty.

There is no discernible pattern in the colourful and frenetic creativity of this period; the chaos was far from exhausted. Alongside glorious ballads there were chilling moral fables, dazzling aphorisms and splendid diary entries. Brecht made several attempts at writing short stories too. I can remember some erotic novellas for example. There was one about Holofernes and Judith, in which Judith is driven to her heroic deed by the disgustingly sweaty feet of the sleeping king – from whose embrace 'she steals at first light'. There was another about the *The Butter-Hoarder*, who is raped by the farm-hand and then reels home in the half-light still clutching the basket of butter she has begged for her fiancé at the front. On 2 December Brecht read me large parts of a thrilling buccaneer story, which proves that he had already been working on 'Bargan'.[6]

Brecht's exceptional musical gifts enabled him to compose folk melodies for almost all his poems, and it seems very plausible, as some people suggest, that many of Weill's or Dessau's compositions can be traced back to Brecht's own ideas. One day, when I brought him one of the serenades I had written for our nightly sessions, he responded with a spontaneous rendition of an improvised guitar accompaniment.

The idea soon came to him that one should revivify opera and operetta too, both of which he saw as quite wrongly neglected markets for lyric poetry. In order to smuggle modern poetry into uncultured households we even came up with the idea of editions on toilet-rolls. We also toyed with the potential of film. In this medium one could, for example, permit one's hero, who might be

---

5. The German title, *Meine Achillesverse*, plays on 'Verse' (verses) and 'Ferse' (heel).
6. 'Bargan gives up', in *Short Stories*, pp. 3–15.

hopelessly cornered in a high-walled courtyard, simply to take off vertically through the air and escape. Ideas like these anticipate modern developments by several decades; none the less, Brecht stuck pretty closely to real life in his work for the theatre. He was quite surprised to find that his ideas were much more revolutionary in every other art-form than in his own – where, for all the innovations, he was basically quite conservative. Now and again his poems make excursions into the surreal and the absurd. I remember a decidedly experimental draft of the 'Anna Cloudface' ballad. The lover, seeking his lost one, suddenly realizes, for no apparent reason, that she is 'in Madagascar'. The jungle associations continue with images of primeval swamps from which a woman emerges – it is all like some vision of prehistoric times. In the psalm-poems too there are many passages which come close to the absurd. Of all these poems, the only one which has been published so far is the Cas Neher poem in Enzensberger's *Museum*.[7] Because he has run out of blue paint, the artist decides to daub the violet skies of Peshawar white. Seven coolies hold up the canvas, and fourteen the inebriated artist. Finally the tricolour masterpiece, which is painted on the interior wall of a sloop, sinks into the depths in a storm. Neher survives. The picture is his pride and joy; for it could never be sold.

Ideas and drafts followed one upon the other in bewildering profusion, and Brecht prevailed upon his friends to immerse themselves in artistic activity too. There was talk of forcing Orge Pfanzelt to sit down and write a book, without any clear idea of a theme. Bert quite seriously suggested to me that we should publish our poems jointly. There was also a plan for a drama in which he wanted to participate, but only in an advisory capacity. It was to be a play full of scoundrels and whores, with just one pure, innocent youth. Otto Bezold composed a few poems and a quite excellent novella, with which Brecht was very impressed, in the style of Maupassant's *La Mort du Manuel Linde*. Of Cas Neher, whose abilities were beyond all doubt, Brecht daily

7. 'Von einem Maler', in *Museum der modernen Poesie*, selected and introduced by Hans Magnus Enzensberger, Frankfurt, 1960 ('About a Painter', *Poems*, pp. 11–12).

demanded new illustrations. At times the walls of the attic in Bleichstraße were completely covered with them. Brecht sought out friends with musical talents too and showered them with librettos and exposés. In his turn, he willingly accepted all our suggestions and corrections to his own work. Occasionally he was even able to turn one of our failed poetic efforts into an excellent composition of his own. Once, when we showed him a piece of schoolboy doggerel called 'Tarpeia', which smacked suspiciously of Felix Dahn,[8] he took up the material and transformed it into a wonderful ballad which began with the words:

> Rome closed her gates. There was no other change.
> Daytime and nighttime. Eating. Sleeping. Breeding.
> No other change disturbed the sleeping city.

I hope and believe that I was able to contribute something to Brecht's work here or there, or at least to encourage him with my interest. Already, even in these early days, there were the beginnings of a collective endeavour – in which Brecht's leadership remained, of course, unchallenged.

8. Felix Dahn (1834–1912), a university professor who wrote conscientiously detailed historical novels about the Germanic and Roman past.

A Conversation   **Publishing Problems**

Towards the end of June 1919 I was preoccupied with the
business of passing my leaving examination and moving to Pasing, so my daily meetings with Brecht in Augsburg had to stop.
Of course we met in Munich, and occasionally, when I could
afford it, I went back home to visit him. Cultural life on the banks
of the Lech seemed so many miles away that I heard nothing at all
of Brecht's vitriolic assaults on the routine boredom of the town
theatre, which he launched as reviewer for the *Volkswille*.[1]
Evidently the only thing our great maestro of the theatre learnt
from this particular establishment was how *not* to run a theatre. A
second theatre, which had opened in Augsburg on the
Schießgraben in the summer of 1919, may perhaps have provided
some inspiration – although perhaps only because of its knock-
about amateurism. After a rather bad production of Wedekind's
Lulu, there was a version of a 'whodunnit' translated from the
English, which had already been very successful in several other
German towns and under several different titles. In Augsburg it
was called *Mister Wu or the Revenge of the Chinaman*.[2] The play
was undemanding to a fault, and not without moments of unintentional humour. As far as I remember, the plot told of a rich
Chinaman's devious designs to bump off his hated son-in-law, in
the course of which, by some mischance, he just happened to lose
his own life. Brecht went to see this box-office hit twice and tried
to persuade his friends to go too. It seems to me quite possible
that this fundamentally worthless spectacle was one of the inspirations for *In the Jungle of Cities*. There is perhaps a pointer to

1. See pp. 160–2.
2. *Mr Wu* may have been Brecht's first encounter with an oriental stage-
set. According to material in the Raymond Mander and Joe Mitchenson
Theatre Collection (to which we are most grateful for this information),
Mr Wu by H. M. Vernon and Harold Owen was first performed in the
Strand Theatre, London, in 1913.

Brecht's interest in the well-known photograph of Karl Valentin's 'Oktoberfest' orchestra, which features Brecht playing the clarinet. On the front of the stall hangs a poster with the title 'Mister Wau Wau'.

The success of *Mister Wu* introduced Brecht to another theatre and to further inspirations. The Augsburg ensemble was invited to take its production to the Blumensäle in Munich for several weeks – a rare event indeed. And in this same building, opposite what is now a high-rise block, there were two autumn premières. Both of them were stories from Bavarian history which Brecht adored and which I also went to see at his suggestion. One of the plays, apparently written by a certain Kleinholz, was called *Ludwig II* and told the fate of the fairytale king – the intrigues against him, his disinvestiture, imprisonment and death. It was out-and-out sensationalism with all the trimmings: recreant lackeys, a repugnant camarilla, ambitious pretenders, and a sad dearth of loyal subjects. The performance was full of life; the noble Count Dürkheim, who defends his king to the last, was greeted with storms of applause, and when Ludwig was ambushed in Neuschwanstein Castle and dragged off to Berg the whole audience wailed and sobbed. In Act Four, just as the people were about to rise up and free their king, there was a moment of high drama: a death knell rang out from Castle Berg signalling the mysterious death of the king. To conclude there was a comic epilogue between the future Ludwig III and Maria Theresa, his wife, with the funeral bells intoning in the background: 'Reserl, now it's yer ain chance to be queen.' 'I ne'er wanted that, as God is m' witness.' 'Get along wi'ye, Reserl, yer canna kid me.'

The second play was called *Novemberstürme* (*November Storms*). The first act was entitled 'A pleasant audience' and was set in the palace: the lord mayor offered his humble thanks for a generous gift of five hundred marks, and then there was a rather foolish confusion of identity in which the king mistook Possart for the roof-mender and the roof-mender for Possart. The second act consisted of an Independent Social Democrat meeting, with speeches by Eisner and a Russian delegate. In the third act the revolution erupted and the king fled. If these three acts were bad, then the fourth was even worse: it was set in heaven, where Eisner finally gained admission and was hailed as Kurt I, despite all the attempts to block his election by a celestial management committee.

The Blumensäle was a theatre where smoking was permitted, like the clubs where Valentin used to appear. Everywhere there were little tables, even up on the gallery, where the audience could sit in comfort or else lounge on the parapet if they became particularly engrossed in the spectacle. People ate, drank beer and smoked. The plays were designed to provoke political reflection, and each act had its own title; one way and another there were many impulses which later were to feed into Brecht's own stagecraft.

Some of the inspirations and ideas from 1919 were to influence Brecht right up until the end. All in all it was a good year, perhaps the most productive of Brecht's life. What was lacking was recognition. Brecht's efforts to have *Spartacus* and *Baal* performed came to nothing. He did not even succeed in having them printed. In June 1919 he delivered a fully revised version of *Baal* to the Musarion publishing house but they sent it back by return, accompanied by a curt, offhand note. At the end of July he was overjoyed to receive the news that the play had been accepted by Dreimasken publishers, and he sent a telegram to Feuchtwanger who had helped with all the negotiations: 'Life is good. Many thanks!' But only a few days later they wriggled out of their offer with some pretty dubious excuses. This series of disappointments and misunderstandings continued into the next year; indeed things got even worse. At the same time we were confronted by the urgent expenses of day-to-day life, to such an extent that around the turn of the year Brecht even appears to have thought seriously about taking up his medical studies again. I heard about some of his most pressing concerns only many years later. There is a song which hints at one of the problems, one which he kept a secret even from the rest of the family: namely the pregnancy of his girlfriend, Bi.[3]

3. See pp. 151–5.

The days of all your bitternesses
are all but over now, my dear,
like those of our illicit kisses
which all too soon will disappear.

Soon life will merely be symbolic,
and even death will just seem cheap,
it won't be long and you'll be catholic
and in the hallowed dirt you'll sleep.

Perhaps I should mention here, for those unfamiliar with the Augsburg idiom, that 'to make someone catholic' means to force someone to their knees, and 'to become catholic' means to submit, or even to forsake this earthly life.

Of course I too had to put all my efforts into the serious business of earning a living, but all the same the two of us managed to meet quite often during the winter term. Brecht and Neher came to visit, and saw all the important theatre productions – from up in the gods of course, where it only cost a few pfennigs and you could just glimpse the actors' feet, though little else. My diary also recounts our visits to the circus, and a visit to the cinema where we watched the great mongoloid, Baal-like Paul Wegener in *The Galley Slave*, an adaptation of Balzac's *Vautrin*.

There are three surviving letters from the spring of 1920, which Brecht spent in Augsburg. For all their apparent equanimity, they betray something of the troubles which beset us.

Augsburg, 24 March 1920

Dear Hanns Otto,

I've just read about your father's death and I wanted to hold your hand. I'm trying to think what I should write, but I can't find words so I'll just hold your hand. A malevolent star presided over our last meeting. Aren't you coming to Augsburg sometime? You could stay the night with us. I'll be back in Munich at the beginning of May.

Best wishes,

Yours, Bert Brecht.   (*Briefe*, p. 63)

Augsburg, beginning of May 1920

Dear Hanns Otto,

Thank you for your letter. I have greatly sinned, but my heart is contrite, so you must forgive me. I wrote you a card saying I had written you a letter. Then I discovered the letter under a pile of papers; but by that time I had mislaid the card, and now both of them are unsent. Time has gone by – you know how it is – and both notes have been languishing in the corner like two rotten eggs – any excuse not to write! The demon in me laughed, just like last time when we were in Munich together, when we parted in Perusastraße because Hedda wanted to go to the opera. I let you go, and then I was sorry and I left her standing and ran after you, and at Starnberger station I heard the train was an hour late and you had nowhere to go. That fault is nagging away in the corner too. But now you must forgive me; it won't happen again. Next week I'm coming to Munich, I hope I'll see you then. I don't know yet where I'll be living, but Hedda Kuhn is staying c/o Däumling at 42 Adalbertstraße.

Thanks again. I press your hand.

Bert.   (*Letters*, p. 60)

Dear Hanns Otto,

Here I am, sitting on my lonely island. It is pleasant here, and here I'll stay until I've grazed it barren. Now and then I take a potshot at the startled birds and gobble them down. Now and then I give the heavens a fresh coat of paint, flea-coloured or embahuba-tree brown, and sometimes I play with Buja Bu the billiard-boy up in the attic.

I'm looking forward to seeing you again soon.

Bert Brecht   (*Letters*, p. 60)

The intimate tone of these letters cannot disguise the real state of affairs. For most of Brecht's old cronies the summer of 1920 was a difficult period, and many a good friendship was to founder for good. Brecht was desperate for success, so it is perfectly comprehensible that his first priority was to establish contact with journalists and writers. In due course they became almost his only companions. One day he was so over-polite when we parted company after one of my visits to Schwabing that I could not help but remember the old Brechtian adage: that it is one's enemies whom one must treat with the greatest courtesy. I came to the conclusion that I did not mean anything to him any longer, and I did not want to be a burden to him. A great and profound friendship seemed to have come to an end.

Brecht himself probably realized the dubious nature of some of his new acquaintances. Many in the long run probably did him more harm than good. Scandalmongers even claimed that there had been a fight in Johst's house on the Starnberger lake, and that faced with the burly Johst our poet had taken up ju-jitsu. Anyway, at the end of November Brecht turned up again out of the blue with his girlfriend, and of course I received him with open arms. A pale light on the horizon seemed to herald a new dawn: at last, or so we believed, *Baal* had found a home with the publisher Georg Müller. We were exhilarated and full of hope. We broke into song, and Brecht started bubbling over with new ideas. He imagined for example how his grandchild might come home from school and ask him, 'Grandad, is it true what the teacher says, that you're such a swine?' 'Your teacher is quite right,' he would then reply, 'I really am a swine' – but the little child would then get nothing for Christmas. Or we imagined scenarios of great men in very human situations: Napoleon eating ice-cream, Jesus with a toothache, or the sublime Dante peeling onions with Beatrice.

Unfortunately Brecht's hopes of success proved illusory once more. With his sights on the stage Brecht had been putting together the version of *Baal* now familiar from later publications. This was considerably shorter than the original, but also artistically inferior. The only addition was a final scene – perhaps the version published in the *Stücke* (*Plays*) or something similar – in which, many years later when Baal's name is mentioned, the foresters have no recollection of him. As far as I remember, however, the scene was cut at the last minute, in order to leave open the ambiguity of Baal's death, or 'non-death'. The publishers had long since set up type for this version when they became entangled in a law-suit about an edition of *Faublas*.[4] The directors began to get worried about *Baal* too, since the play has several openly erotic scenes. They wanted at all costs to avoid any more interference by the public prosecutor, so they withdrew from the contract and surrendered the compositor's work to the author. Willy Haas's account,[5] that old Müller himself happened to stumble upon the page-proof and kicked up a fuss, is not particularly likely. Müller died in December 1917 – and there is no reason to suppose that he was still busy haunting the offices years after his death. In any case, the task which confronted us now was to come up with another publisher. He would only need to finance the print-run itself. Brecht was even prepared to supply the paper – by way of the Haindl factory – which in times like these was no mean thing. However, no one was to be found who would take the risk. Among others, I approached Heinrich Franz Bachmair, a close acquaintance who had been the first to publish J. R. Becher, but he too refused. Several of Brecht's other manuscripts were offered to Bachmair and, as he was planning another series of luxury editions, I tried to persuade him at least to undertake a separate edition of the 'Ballad of the pirates' with Neher's illustrations. Unfortunately he rejected this suggestion, for which I already had Brecht's consent; and a special edition of the 'Legend of the dead soldier', which Bachmair was seriously considering, did not meet with Brecht's approval. Once again, all our plans had come to nothing.

For this particular year the bibliography of Brecht's publications contains only theatre reviews. His contributions to the Augsburg *Volkswille* have nearly all been made accessible to scholarship. However, on days when there were two important cultural events, Brecht was in Munich, standing in for Lion Feuchtwanger. For example, I can definitely remember a discussion of Carl Sternheim's *Marquise von Arcis* which was performed

4. *Les Amours du Chevalier de Faublas*, an erotic novel by Louvet de Couvray (1760–97).
5. See Bibliography.

in the Residenztheater on 11 December 1920. The name of the
newspaper – in which there may well be a whole series of Brecht
reviews – now escapes me. It seems to have been a quite short-
lived publication; all efforts to trace it have failed. I only recall
how we collected the press copies from the union house in
Pestalozzistraße, just a stone's throw from Brecht's own lodgings.
I believe there was an office of the Independent Social Democrats
in the same building. Brecht's article opened with the Miezzi-
Krummbach verses:

> Working in the Institute in town,
> he shivered in a cellar dank and airless,
> Washing all those bloody corpses down
> and shoving them inside the furnace.
>
> The furnace didn't give off warmth, instead
> an icy blast which set one's teeth to chatter.
> Once the vital parts were frozen rigid,
> to dissect them was an easy matter.

This, Brecht argued, had been Sternheim's practice too. He had
exhumed one of Diderot's literary cadavers, prepared it and strip-
ped it down himself, all the flesh had been pared away, and now it
rattled horribly in all its joints and hinges. The review was signed
'Bert Brecht', and underneath Feuchtwanger had added: 'We
booed *The Drawers*[6] off the stage, this is the Sternheim we
deserve.' Brecht handed me the newspaper with the ironic
remark: 'Here you have it – Brecht in print.' It was by no means
the case that publishers rushed to tear the manuscripts from
under the poet's pen, as Brüstle claims.[7] All of Brecht's marvellous poems had already been written by now, but none of them
had appeared in any of the important newspapers and periodicals
of the time.

In the winter of 1920–1 I often met up with Brecht again. In

6. *Die Hose* (*The Drawers*), one of Carl Sternheim's most famous com-
edies, first performed in 1911 as *Der Riese* (*The Giant*), a concession to
the Berlin police chief who had forbidden public performance on moral
grounds.
7. See Bibliography.

December he introduced me to the young Otto Zarek in whose parental home in Berlin, almost a year later, Brecht and Bronnen were to meet.[8] On 15 February we attended Georg Kaiser's trial, for which Brecht had obtained press tickets. Legally speaking it was an open-and-shut case: a patron had put his villa at Kaiser's disposal and Kaiser had secretly been selling valuables from it in order to keep himself and his family. What was really disgraceful was the way the author had spent twenty-three days being dragged in chains from prison to prison with two convicted criminals for company, all the way from Berlin to Munich. Kaiser gave a stirring final address. The man and poet Kaiser, or so he said, had been his theme that morning; his last request was that the court should hear two witnesses for the defence, who could not, however, appear in person: 'I am referring, of course, to my departed brothers, Heinrich von Kleist and Georg Büchner.' Their spirit was in him, he said, from them he had received the flaming torch, and it was his duty to keep that flame alive. Bronnen confirms that Brecht had a high opinion of Kaiser early on, though he probably only ever approached the artificiality of Kaiser's sometimes barren dramas much later, in the period of the *Lehrstücke*.[9]

My diary contains extensive jottings from a conversation with Brecht when I visited him at home in Augsburg at the beginning of January. They can probably only be understood if we remember that Brecht was very depressed at the time. There are gloomy reflections about our age and especially about the future of art, which frequently read like a refutation of Brecht's usual attitudes. It seemed remarkable to him, or at least symptomatic of the age, that the things we took seriously, and indeed had to take seriously, were things that formerly we would have just laughed about. He confidently predicted the demise of poetry, which he saw as the ineluctable consequence of the abrogation of tradition. According to these ideas his own former belief in the future had been merely a naive error. Truly great art, he maintained, was only possible in an age of conservatism and prosperity, such as might permit that enjoyment of simplicity which we experience in

8. See p. 169–70.   9. Brecht's 'learning plays' of the years 1929–34.

Shakespeare. I doubt however that Brecht was already oppressed
by a sense that, in the coming 'dark times', 'a conversation about
trees' would almost be a crime because it would imply a 'silence
about so many horrors'; and he had definitely not yet arrived at
his later conviction that even in the dark times there would still be
singing – 'about the dark times'.[10] Rather, he recognized that,
although a gifted writer might indeed be able to attain the highest
poetic distinction in periods of traditional values, he would be
hard pressed in periods of transition to create truly great and
lasting works. Above all, Brecht maintained, we were without
those essential precursors who would hurl themselves into the
abyss so that their successors could clamber over their corpses to
greatness – as Marlowe had done for Shakespeare. The pioneering
achievement of Wedekind, whose *Wetterstein* trilogy might have
been similarly significant for the present generation, had not yet
been fully recognized. We were inclined not to see beyond the
witty façade. The success of Wedekind's *Lulu* was dependent on
characters such as Schigolch and Rodrigo Quast, who in fact
could only compromise the greatness of the play. Of course
Wedekind himself bore some of the responsibiliy, for he had
distracted our gaze from the broader contours of his drama with
'red curtains and paprika schnitzels'.

Brecht was going through a phase of almost puritanical strin-
gency. As yet he did not perceive the theatre as an instrument of
political didacticism, but he did agree with Schiller that it should
be a place of moral instruction. The author of the *Summer
Symphony* was beginning to sound like a moral apostle. He criti-
cized the sultry atmosphere of such harmlessly amusing novels as
Faublas, he even defended the confiscation of the new edition of
Louvet de Couvray with Walser's illustrations, and he utterly
condemned the work of Gustav Sack, whose novel *Ein verbum-
melter Student* (*A Dissolute Student*) had much moved me.[11]

Around the turn of the year, despite this mood, he threw

10. See Brecht's poems written in exile, 'To those born later' and
'Motto', in *Svendborg Poems* (*Poems*, pp. 318–20).
11. Gustav Sack (1885–1916), an early Expressionist writer of violent
and macabre novels and poems.

himself wholeheartedly back into work on his old comedy *Geigei* or *Galigay*. Originally it has been called *Green Garraga*, perhaps a reference to Tirso de Molina's *Don Gil of the Green Breeches*, and years later it was to be staged under the title *Man equals Man*. The play has of course suffered many different interpretations: at the Berlin première they were struck by its anti-militarism, whereas Ernst Schumacher[12] has pointed out echoes of Marx–Engels's theory of the depersonalization of the proletariat, an idea which was part of the political culture of post-Second World War socialist Germany. Of course ideas like this were later worked into it, but they had nothing to do with the original conception. Brecht's intention was simply to demonstrate how a man goes out to buy a fish, and then – simply because he cannot say no – gets caught up in an affair which has nothing to do with him, eventually finds there can be no turning back, is swallowed by the machinery of war, and finally disappears in the Indian campaign. A prologue warns of the dangers of being kind-hearted: one should always consider the possible consequences, in order to avoid the fate, '. . . which only yesterday/befell green Garraga, they say'.

The first scene was already complete; it showed Galigay getting ready for the market and asking his wife, like some Karl Valentin character, exactly what size and manner of fish she desires. The sequence in the temple was also finished, the break-in, the failed attempt to release Jip, and the introduction of the new god with whose help the impoverished owner of the 'yellow men's pagoda' hopes to improve his financial circumstances. The events in the camp were still in their first stages. The most impressive figure, next to Widow Begbick, was Sergeant Bloody Five, who was called John-I-am-happy in these early drafts. I can remember one scene in which the soldiers make fun of their terrible sergeant:

John-I-am-happy slept in the sea-dogs' bar
and played at poker and drank,
and when he had bet his soul away
they gave him a sergeant's rank.

12. See Bibliography.

John-I-am-happy,
who's your mother, hey?
Black bastards, I'll be sworn
have no one who will mourn
for them, come Judgement Day!
To which he then did say:
John-I-am-happy was born
to his Mama Army – okay?!

Whenever old Bloody Five gets into impossible difficulties he is
snatched from the brink of disaster by an unlikely promotion:
first of all he becomes a corporal, eventually even a commissar.
The confidence the three looters feel after their successful disguis-
ing of Galigay, which gives rise to this little song, turns out,
however, to be ill-founded. In the midst of their games, the
silhouette of their prowling tormentor appears on the tent wall
and their song breaks off in mid-sentence.

The execution of this outwardly simple plot was beset with
serious difficulties; there was the danger of a sort of fairy-tale
improbability. It was particularly difficult to make plausible the
transformation of a harmless packer into a frenzied beserk
without compromising Galigay's individuality. Brecht was even
moved to ask himself if his protagonist could be considered
human at all. For here it was not a question of one man's submis-
sion to a mass psychology; rather it was the abrupt transformation
of a single psyche and a single social function. Surprisingly, we
never got around to discussing how Galigay's individuality might
already have been eroded by his occupation as a packer, in line
with Marx's ideas about the consequences of working under
capitalism. Instead, Brecht drew attention to the inescapable
forces operating on his hero; he argued that his antagonists too
were subject to such duress that they might have had no alternative but to throw Galigay into the river. The result of all the
intricacies of the play could only ever be to reveal 'the untruth,
but never the truth'.

I did not find any of this very convincing, and so Brecht was
forced to explain all his notions about freedom and determinism.

Imagine my surprise when Brecht came out with all kinds of astrological mumbo-jumbo, in order – supposedly – to justify a mechanistic understanding of the human race. He reckoned that the earth should be understood as a magnetic field governed by the stars, so that world history and even the smallest individual fate must follow a pre-ordained path. He went so far as to claim that the heart was driven by magnetism; and some close Socratic questioning on my part coaxed from him the confession that he did indeed believe in a form of absolute determinism. He perceived phenomena such as prophecy and second sight as proof of his theories.

Such opinions, which would surely imply some concept of fate as the governing principle of drama, might seem strange in the mouth of a playwright who was later so concerned to illustrate that society, the environment and the whole course of human history were subject to man's intervention. He was later to stress that the actions demonstrated by his players on stage were just one of several possible and freely available responses to a situation. In these early years Brecht was evidently still prone to some pretty violent swings of opinion. But it is no accident that, shortly afterwards, he became a stern opponent of Alfred Döblin's theory of the novel, although it actually has a certain amount in common with his own later 'epic theatre'. According to Döblin, the arrangement of the individual parts could be compared to the segments of an earthworm. Brecht, on the other hand, was convinced that the individual parts must be an organic sequence, and he concluded his rejection of the 'earthworm theory' with the remark that you can have a 'Goldregen' and a 'Regenwurm', but never a 'Goldregenwurm'.[13] These deterministic ideas cannot have persisted all that long. None the less, it is perfectly likely that this fatalistic phase was sufficient to impede the development of several of his ongoing literary experiments. In retrospect even that may seem a considerable loss.

13. Brecht uses the words 'Goldregen' (shower of gold, or laburnum) and 'Regenwurm' (earthworm, literally rainworm) to demonstrate that although some meaningful compounds may be created by dislocating and juxtaposing individual parts, a 'goldshowerworm' would, for example, be nonsense.

Strangely enough, I cannot discover a date in my old notes for the *Mahagonny* songs which, despite their verve, show stylistic similarities with the 'John-I-am-happy' song. They probably belong, in part at least, to the same period as *Green Garraga*. The poems included in the *Domestic Breviary* are evidently only a small selection. I can remember at least one other, with the following refrain:

Jenny dear, my dearest Jen,
when can we go to bed?
Jenny sighed, all the other men
are better behaved, she said.

This was one of Brecht's favourites, although it has no particular literary value.

I cannot date the exact beginning of Brecht's work on the dramatization of *Gösta Berling* either. In this case, however, we can derive some impression of his progress from letters to Arnolt Bronnen. I only recall how Brecht recited the entirety of the opening scene, which was composed in irregular rhymed verse. It was a brief but impressive sketch of the arrival of Sintram in the smithy on New Year's Eve, and of the conclusion of the pact with the devil. It seems a great pity that nothing is now known of this dramatization, although it cannot surely all have been lost.[14]

14. The prologue to Brecht's version of Selma Lagerlöf's novel *Gösta Berling's Saga* (1891) was published in January 1924 in the periodical *Das Kunstblatt*. According to Bronnen's account, Brecht abandoned the project at quite a late stage when he ran into copyright problems with Elly Karin, on whose earlier dramatization his own work was based.

1. Bertolt Brecht in 1917

2. From left: Brecht, Otto Müllereisert,
Georg Pfanzelt (standing), Otto Bezold

3. Hanns Otto Münsterer in 1919

4. Brecht playing the clarinet in Karl Valentin's 'Oktoberfest' orchestra, with Liesl Karlstadt in top-hat and Valentin playing the tuba (see p. 88)

5. One of Caspar Neher's drawings of Baal (see pp. 15–16)

6. Paula Banholzer and Brecht, 1918

7. Brecht in Augsburg, 1921

Success   *Drums* and *Zibebe*

Gradually Brecht began to withdraw from Munich and
spend more and more time in Augsburg, until he finally left for
Berlin, and our friendship, which had become very close over the
winter, was interrupted once again. Nobody heard much of
Brecht for a while, except that I read in the press at the beginning
of April 1921 that the 'Apfelböck' ballad had been issued with
sheet-music by Hardy in Worms but had been seized and pulped
even before distribution. The authorities obviously left no stone
unturned – at least I have only ever heard of one copy of it, which
turned up in Hamburg years ago and must have been sold
abroad.[1]

The rumours I heard about Brecht's life in Berlin were no
comfort. Although he had managed to attract the attention of the
critic Jhering, his intended conquest of the capital had been a
failure;[2] not one of the Berlin papers had published any of his
work, and on top of that he was miserably poor. He was admitted
to the Charité suffering from a kidney infection and total exhaus-
tion. All the same, his wit and charm succeeded in making him
new friends even in hospital – despite the fact that when the
doctor in charge of admissions asked him dubiously whether he
had a serious problem, he replied, 'Not as serious as yours!' But
of course it was his friendship with Bronnen which was the talk of
Munich. The two terrible 'B's, Arnolt and Bertolt, had finally
come together. And a letter of January 1922 testifies that he had
many literary projects on the boil:

---

1. Later correspondence between Münsterer and the Brecht Archive
established that this is probably a confusion. Münsterer must have been
thinking of a small Berlin anthology called *Das Bordell: Eine groteske
Publikation*, edited by Fried-Hardy Worm and published in 1921.
2. For further details of life in Berlin, see pp. 169–71.

Dear Hanns Otto,

I was delighted with your present; Berlin is a cold city and at Christmas I spent most of my time getting drunk. I probably won't get home before the spring. Have you got anything suitable for cabaret? Songs, chansons, dramatic monologues? I could certainly sell that sort of stuff here, or get it published in a magazine, etc. Send me a parcel(s?), as much as you can put together! I promise not to cock it up and lose it!

With many grrreetings!

Yours, Bert

Say hello to Bez for me some time, won't you? And write to me with *all* your news.   (*Briefe*, p. 75)

That Brecht's siege of Berlin came to an end in the early summer of 1922 was simply a matter of self-preservation. Prices had begun to soar; for example, an Insel book worth 50 pfennigs in 1912, and listed at 5 marks in the spring catalogue, cost a staggering 1200 marks by the autumn, and was printed on evil-smelling brown paper. Of course the necessities of life were no different.

Sometimes I used to eat out, although that too was something I could rarely afford. I used to go to a tiny grillhouse in Augustenstraße with the highflown name 'Bavaria', where we were treated to a *ragoût* which consisted of a chunk of intestine containing hard knobbly lumps – even a practised pathologist would not have been able to distinguish with any certainty whether they were solidified excrement or caseated tubercles. Only one thing was certain: these delicacies, which cost us a small fortune, must have found their way into the 'Bavaria' from a waste-bucket under the 'operating' slab in the slaughterhouse. The situation cannot have been any better in Berlin. The inflation, first creeping but soon galloping, was disastrous enough for salaried and waged employees, but for freelance writers it was a catastrophe. By the time the royalties finally came dribbling in they would not even buy a bread roll. Brecht's parents' home was the only refuge; besides, Falckenberg was impressed with *Drums in the Night* and it had been accepted by the Munich Kammer-spiele.

On 2 July Brecht and Neher visited me in Pasing. Neher made a sketch of me and my daughter – not that I had one of course, but that was how Neher claimed she would one day look. There is also a sketch for *Drums in the Night* which Neher must have done at the same time. It was Neher who created the first drawings of figures and decorations, and Otto Reigbert, who was the official designer for the Munich performance, bor-rowed many of his ideas – such as the innovative half walls with the town or the moonlit night constantly visible above them. On 29 August I received a card from Brecht calling me over to Leopoldstraße. He was planning a comedy called *Klamauk* (*Rumpus*) and was working on *Hannibal*, which had been inspired by Steinrück's production of Grabbe's play of the same name. The only scene of this play to have appeared in print depicts the crossing of the Alps to the accompaniment of a frenzied drum-beat. I can also recall his final departure scene from Italy: in Grabbe's play, Hannibal falls down and embraces the earth for the last time, in Brecht's he takes a last pee – the same symbolic gesture which in *Edward* takes the place of Gaveston's farewell repast. One of Brecht's comments in a letter to Jhering seems to refer to this.[3] And so the rehearsals of *Drums in the Night* began. Officially Falckenberg was the director, but Brecht intervened to such an extent that there were several severe disagreements. It would often happen that Falckenberg got into a temper; half an hour, even a whole hour, might pass in anxious waiting before someone managed to talk him round and calm him down. I was there for all the rehearsals, and Brecht would constantly solicit suggestions and new ideas – once we had to correct a medical impossibility in the text. In short, this was the first appearance of a 'Brecht team', of which there were later to be many famous examples; at that time I was the only member, and a theatrical outsider at that.

The first performance of *Drums in the Night* took place on

3. 'The voilà at the end is rather offensive, don't you think' (*Letters*, pp. 70).

Friday, 29 September 1922, not on 22 or 23 September, as often claimed. The theatre was packed; we were on tenter hooks and running terribly late. Brecht whispered excitedly that the Berlin critics were all there and that, most significantly, Jhering had arrived.[4] All the Brecht family were there too, his father, Walter, the housekeeper Roecker, and Bi. Everyone assumed I was Brecht's brother. At last, with the audience growing restless, the gong rang out three times, the curtains parted – and the catastrophe took its course. Everything that had been meticulously worked out during the rehearsals and had been perfect only that afternoon at the dress rehearsal went horribly awry. The third act, which had been the very best in rehearsal, was a disaster; and the old theatre superstition, that good rehearsals mean bad premières, once again proved true. The play was nevertheless a great success, thanks to its elemental power and to the language, a language such as had not been heard on the German stage for years. The reviews did not appear until Monday, so there were two whole days of hoping and waiting. When they finally did come out, they were generally very favourable. Brecht could be well pleased with his first success.

Only a day after *Drums in the Night*, on the Saturday, there was a midnight première of *Die rote Zibebe* (*The Red Raisin*), for which Brecht was also named as the author. The name comes from the third act of *Drums in the Night* where the action is set in a tavern called the Red Raisin. There was a semi-circle of wooden huts with curtains at the front, which looked like bathing-cabins. Old Glubb took the part of a mute conférencier; he limped his way over to the cabins one by one and drew back the curtain with a long schoolmaster's cane. The figure inside the cabin trundled stiffly out like an automaton and sang or declaimed his piece. Then, as if the spring had wound down, he would slide backwards into the cabin, and the innkeeper pulled the curtain to. Brecht himself took part in the first performance. Since I was only able to see the second, and final, performance on the Sunday, I shall confine myself to describing that. On this occasion actors and actresses recited or sang Brecht's poems. A large number of

4. See pp. 165–6.

Klabund's[5] verses were performed too, and he himself appeared in a black suit and recited 'Der arbeitslose Totengräber' ('The unemployed gravedigger') in an eerie monotone:

I'll tell you the truth and I'll tell you straight,
we haven't got time to haggle or shirk,
a poor, itinerant digger of graves
is looking for work.
Have you no dead to bury,
no aunt, or no beloved . . .

The idea was to make modern poetry more palatable to the audience by means of a large number of costumes and different voices. The colourlessness of most of Klabund's own poems, however, made the whole thing dreadfully tedious. The second part brought some relief: it comprised a Karl Valentin number, the 'Christmas-tree Cabaret' I think, which had no real connection with the rest of the show. This was preceded by the incredible penny-farthing sketch. Presumably very few people will remember this grotesque piece, so I will set it down here as part and parcel of this 'Brecht-play'. Liesl Karlstadt played the impresario, and announced: 'Act One, three times round the stage on the penny-farthing.' Valentin clambered laboriously onto his antiquated vehicle and circled the stage three times. 'Act Two, three times round the stage on the penny-farthing, with bells.' The same thing happened again, but this time accompanied by Karlstadt swinging a cow-bell. 'Third and Final Act, the death-defying journey through dark and murky night.' After a short but sinister silence – the tension was mounting – Karlstadt set up two poles with a paper banner bearing the legend 'dark and murky night'. Then Valentin wobbled cautiously back and forth a few times, before, eventually, he took a run and burst through the banner. Valentin was crowned with a laurel wreath to tumultuous applause, while Karlstadt presented the paper tatters to the

5. Klabund was the pen-name of Alfred Henschke (1890–1928), the author of several historical novels and of ecstatic Expressionist poetry. He also made adaptations from the Chinese, one of which Brecht later made use of in his *Caucasian Chalk Circle*.

audience as if she were an executioner displaying a guillotined head to the baying crowds.

The Red Raisin represented an attempt to exploit the theatrical space for a literary cabaret. It came to a sudden end when the provisional police licence was withdrawn. The critics all shook their heads that a genuine poet who, only the previous night, had taken them by storm with a splendid play, should have lent his name to such worthless rubbish. And that was the end of that. There is perhaps just one thing to add. Here too Brecht was anticipating future practice in one respect: years later, poetry readings broadcast on the radio would often divide the text amongst several contrasting voices.

Jungle of Cities and Edward

A few observations about *The Red Raisin* bring my diary entries about Brecht to a close; the subsequent pages have been ripped out and all further notes up until 1925 were burnt. I had heard very little from Brecht, so that the première of *The Jungle* on 9 May 1923 came as something of a surprise. The performance began in rousing style, albeit shockingly for the audience of the Residenztheater. Cas Neher's sets were fully visible, turning on an open revolve with the street sounds of the waking city rising above them – until the stage came haltingly to rest, as if by chance, at Mayne's lending library. And in the cries of 'git up' by the Chicago carters there were echoes of Jensen's *The Wheel*, which had been a great influence on the early drafts of the play. Everything went quite well until the interval. The audience in this particular theatre had just about got used to Bahr and Molnár,[1] but, although they felt somewhat alienated, they were not altogether hostile to such an odd plot. Then, as the struggle between Shlink and Garga became increasingly brutal, the performance started to be interrupted by occasional whistles, which eventually became an almost unbroken chorus. The actors carried on bravely, but the general unrest made it virtually impossible to follow the performance. When the curtain finally fell there was a scandal such as this theatre had never seen before: furious cat-calls and whistles, as well as frenzied applause. I remember how my hands were red and smarting for days afterwards. Despite Jhering's enthusiastic praise, the local reviews were devastating, there were ructions in the theatre, and after a few more rowdy performances the play was withdrawn.

All in all I met Brecht very seldom that year. I do remember a

1. Hermann Bahr (1863–1934) and the Hungarian Ferenc Molnár (1878–1952) were prolific and popular contemporary dramatists in Vienna and Munich.

few afternoons spent in the garden-house in Pasing, although I cannot put a precise date on them. One occasion saw the composition of the song of those courageous men who, '. . . in distant Polynesia / singed the Sultan's whiskers'. Later they come under the thumb of their nagging wives: 'Johnny put your tool away, Johnny, don't spit on the blind, heh!' The poem concludes with the lament: 'Forsooth, 'twixt earth and heaven there's no horror can compare / With being forced into wedlock by a creature with long, blonde hair.'

We even wrote poems together. We planned a sort of *Plunderhorn*,[2] which was to parody all the kitsch apparently essential to the German soul. One of the things we completed was a travesty of the well-known folksong about the banks of the Saale, in which we lamented the decline of feudalism and the downfall of the robber barons:

> On the bonny banks of the Saale
> castles stand proud 'gainst the sky
> but no knights their horns are sounding
> and no noble hearts are pounding,
> and the dungeons empty lie.

I can also remember a song about 'A solitary tree in the Odenwald', and another about 'Hauptmann Köpenick', the courageous soldier, 'whom the thankless Republic / has also now forgotten'.[3] The poem tells how he arrives in heaven and everyone wants to take off their hats to him – but alas, in heaven they do not wear hats. Eventually, just one compassionate angel takes pity on the poor wretch. He gives up his free Sunday afternoons to stand for hours in front of the Hauptmann, stiffly saluting 'as if

2. An intended anthology of parodies, modelled on *Des Knaben Wunderhorn* (*The Boy's Magic Horn*), a famous collection of German folksongs compiled by Achim von Arnim and Clemens Brentano (1805–8).
3. An episode in Berlin in 1906 formed the factual basis for this story. A poor ex-convict disguised himself as a captain ('Hauptmann') and on the strength of his uniform was able to commandeer soldiers and raid the town-hall in Köpenick. The most famous literary treatment of this is Carl Zuckmayer's satire on German militarism, *Der Hauptmann von Köpenick* (1931).

turned to a pillar of stone'. Thus even the captain achieves heavenly contentment. This was of course one of Brecht's great misjudgements; the up-and-coming spirit of German militarism could not be palmed off with mere civilian honours.

For the first few months of 1924 we were apparently very close again. I sat, a solitary spectator in the auditorium, through all the rehearsals for *Edward*, which fortunately enough fell during the university vacation. This time Brecht himself was officially named as director. He used the rehearsals to work through all kinds of possibilities on stage, and in cases of doubt he would turn to me for the final judgement. For example, I was expected to judge whether, in the scene in parliament where the peers demand the signature from the defeated king, it would be more effective for them to push the table towards him in one movement, or inch by inch. The performance, which took place on 18 March, was once again both a fiasco and a success. Neher's ramshackle medieval setting was fantastic and completely did away with any cliché romanticism. Faber was excellent;[4] Mortimer was drunk; and it was not a very good idea to have young Edward, whose first royal act was to hang, draw and quarter the traitors, played by a girl . . . but Rudolf Frank has already given a detailed account of this in his *Spielzeit meines Lebens* (*My Theatrical Life*). In my opinion, however, the greatest problem was the scene changes, which were so badly organized that the play dragged on until almost midnight. Yet it was still a success. I wrote a piece about it for the Augsburg papers, and prepared another about Brecht's poetry, designed to coincide with the publication of the *Domestic Breviary*. My essays must have captured something of the spirit of his undertaking – at least Brecht told me that I was the only person who had really understood him. A third article, written for the Magdeburg newspaper, was held ready for publication for two whole years, but was never published. The brown stormclouds of National Socialism were gathering on the horizon. With Brecht's move to Berlin we gradually grew further apart, although there was never a formal break. The last time I saw

4. Erwin Faber played Edward. For further explanation of the following passage, see pp. 167–8.

Brecht before his emigration was in 1926 when he visited Augsburg; a copy of the *Pocket Breviary*, which I carefully guarded and even hid in the rafters of a village church during the bombings, remains a precious souvenir of that visit.

Twenty-five Years Later

My reunion with Brecht after his return from exile does not really belong to this account. What I had once foretold had come to pass: Brecht had not merely become one of the greatest, but also one of the most celebrated writers of all time. However, this had created such a gulf between the two of us that now I could not even think of trying to approach him.

The impulse to do so came from Marieluise Fleißer, who knew of my undiminished respect for the poet and had obviously mentioned it to him.[1] I hesitated for a long time before accepting Brecht's invitation to meet. One often reads about the reunion of friends after a long separation – Lotte and Goethe, Verlaine and Rimbaud. Such meetings can be cold and distant. I was apprehensive. It is a symptom of Brecht's singular human qualities in later years that, when we did meet, it took just a few short minutes to rediscover the genuine warmth of our long gone youth. Day after day, or at least as often as my professional commitments would permit, I attended the rehearsals for *Mother Courage* and was once more together with Brecht. One of my last great joys, and indeed a particular honour, was the brief hour that the poet spent with me on the very day of the première. A few of my most recent poems earned Brecht's honest praise, 'Engel der Versuchung' ('Angel of temptation'), 'Wägung der Zehntausend' ('Judgement of the ten thousand') and 'Fest der Hirten' ('Shepherds' celebration'). Before my return to Berlin, I received a handwritten note, thanking me 'for many kindnesses':

1. Fleißer (1901–74) was herself a talented playwright who allowed herself and her literary aspirations to be eclipsed, first by her association with Brecht in the early years in Munich (see p. 155) then in a bourgeois marriage. She only came to prominence again in the nineteen sixties, when she was something of a mentor to Rainer Werner Fassbinder and others. Like Münsterer, she died in 1974.

> In the dark times
> will there also be singing?
> Yes, there will also be singing
> about the dark times.

I saw my friend once more, at a production of *The Good Person of Szechwan*. We had only a few minutes together, but promised ourselves more time in the autumn. When I asked him how he was, he answered, 'Tired, very tired.'

On New Year's Eve of 1955 to 1956, in the middle of the night, I was suddenly filled with the certainty that I should never see Brecht again. As far as I knew, he was in the best of health, and since I myself had symptoms of a bout of influenza I thought it must be that my own hour was approaching. And so, at the turning of the year, I sat down to write a letter, a simple and unsentimental letter, thanking Brecht for everything he had meant to me and given me. It was intended as a last word of friendship, and that is really all it was; thanks from one friend to another, which I did not want to take with me to the grave, unspoken. It all came about quite differently. Death spared the little life, and took the irreplaceable one.

Further Perspectives

I

The Family in Augsburg

Augsburg lies outstretched on a ridge of ground, rising up in the midst of a distantly wooded plain and bordered in the north by the converging mountain rivers, the Lech and the Wertach. The fine and evenly proportioned silhouette presented by the towers of its distinctive monuments and buildings can be seen for miles: the Cathedral in the north, the Perlach Tower and Rathaus in the centre, and St Ulrich's in the south.   (Walter Brecht, pp. 10–11)*

Augsburg is a rural town steeped in two thousand years of history. It still proudly bears the marks of its former existences as an Imperial City of the Holy Roman Empire and erstwhile capital of the Fugger banking house. Walter Brecht tells of his and his elder brother's early love for both the legends and the monuments of the city. Marianne Zoff reports how Brecht led her back and forth across Augsburg until her feet ached, exploring every nook and cranny, and trying to impress her with his exhaustive knowledge of its history (*So viel wie eine Liebe*, p. 158). The dismissive and rather peevish remarks about the provincial boredom of the place, which Brecht made just after his arrival in Berlin, are well known (e.g. pp. 25–6). However, one should not underestimate his long-standing affection for Augsburg, nor the stimuli which were provided by the atmosphere of this, his home town.

The Brecht family lived just outside the medieval city walls in the Klaucke suburb, adjoining the banks of the Lech, the river meadows and the town moat. In 1954, recalling the genesis of one of his early plays, *In the Jungle of the Cities*, Brecht describes the atmosphere.

I wrote the play very largely out of doors while walking. An alley of Spanish chestnuts ran parallel with the old city moat past my father's house; beyond it were the wall and the remnants of the fortifications.

*See Abbreviations (pp. xv–xvi) for details of the texts quoted in 'Further Perspectives'.

Swans swam on the still, green water. The chestnuts were shedding
their yellow leaves. The paper I wrote on was thin typing paper,
folded in four to fit inside my leather notebook.

('On Looking through my first plays', *Collected Plays*, p. 349)

His younger brother remembers:

Our home territory consisted of the Klaucke suburb and the Klaucke
meadow with the Stadtbach running through it, but home itself was
of course number 2 Bleichstraße, the first in a row of four identical
two-storey houses . . .

The four houses were not particularly attractive, although they did
have some classical features. Somebody once complained that the
regularly spaced houses of this grey row lacked any kind of individuality [compare pp. 7–8]. They seemed individual enough to us
because we knew the people who lived in them, and all the families,
each one different from the next. Their attitude towards us boys was
friendly and respectful, as befitted the sons of the administrator of
the estate – for that was our father's position.

(Walter Brecht, pp. 44–5)

Their father was a director of the Haindl paperworks and the
administrator of this row of houses – built in 1880 by Elise Haindl
in memory of her husband and intended for the deserving poor,
particularly amongst the Haindl employees. Although clearly set
apart from their neighbours by their social status, the young boys
were fascinated by the daily life of this workers' quarter. Many
years later, in exile in Denmark, Brecht was to remember the
Klaucke suburb in a short poem:

A spring evening in the outskirts.
The four houses of the estate
Look white in the dusk.
The workmen are still sitting
At the dark tables in the yard.
They talk of the yellow peril.
A few little girls go for beer
Although the brass bell of the Ursuline convent has already
                                                        rung.
In shirtsleeves their fathers lean over the window sills.
Their neighbours wrap the peach trees on the house walls
In little white rags against the night frost.

('Nature Poem' II, *Poems*, p. 272)

Much of Brecht's life in Bleichstraße was dominated by his mother's worsening illness, which Münsterer also mentions. Before long she became completely housebound, and Eugen was moved upstairs to the now famous attic room so as to accommodate a housekeeper, Marie Roecker, the constant companion to his mother.

Those warm summer afternoons we were still able to carry mother into the garden where she would lie on a divan and talk with visitors and us brothers, or read in the shade of the summer-house. When she became bedridden her life was confined to the back room of the apartment, one window overlooking the garden with its trees and bushes, the other over the little garden between our house and the next.

When we came home late from the theatre, from a concert or from evenings spent with friends, we would see a light still burning in her room. So we knew that she had lain awake for hours. We silently reproached ourselves for having left her alone . . . We crept indoors and took care to close the doors without a sound.

(Walter Brecht, p. 262)

Brecht's guests used to pay their respects to his mother on their way up to his attic retreat. Hedda Kuhn, a friend from Brecht's university days in Munich, recalls seeing her 'always in great pain and under the calming influence of morphine' (*Brecht in Augsburg*, p. 158).

After years of suffering, Frau Brecht's condition became critical in the spring of 1920. Walter records:

On the evening of the first of May all the windows were flung wide open. The three great chestnut trees stood holding their pale candelabra aloft in the gathering dusk. The scent of spring came into the room. On this evening mother was asleep, and, without any apparent change, she died in that sleep, quiet, as she had always been.

Later we were standing in the living room. Not a word was said. But we three, Papa, Eugen and I, felt closer than ever before. At other times some shadow of authority had always intervened between the father and his sons, in that moment it yielded to a silent and unifying grief.

(Walter Brecht, p. 348–9)

The expression of that grief, however, left the family once more divided in its incomprehension. Walter remembers with horror his brother's reaction:

> The evening after our mother's death he invited his friends up to the attic. They made just as much racket as ever. Who knows what they must have felt as they looked on at his extravagant behaviour, a behaviour which scorned any public expression of emotion. Who knows what made him do this in his grief. We others in the house were mute with pain.   (Walter Brecht, p. 350)

An echo of the complex emotional relationship between Brecht and his mother was to find its way into his early writing. Several of his first anti-war poems focus on the pain of the soldiers' mothers: 'Modern legend', 'Mothers of the missing'. After her death Brecht expressed some of this mixture of guilt, anger and devotion in a series of moving notebook entries and poems.

> Since yesterday evening my mother has been dead, her hands grew slowly colder while she was still breathing, she spoke nothing more, she just stopped breathing.

> My pulse is a bit quicker, I can still see clearly, can walk, I had my supper. [Fragment, 2 May 1920]

> They were just bones they laid in a sheet. He left before the earth had covered her over. Why watch an inescapable routine? [May 1920]

> One sees some ordinary person and says: 'My mother, for instance, was never, not for one minute of her life, never once so healthy as that. That's just part of it.'

> My mother:
> I loved her in my way, but she wanted to be loved in her own way.
>   (*Tagebücher*,* pp. 196–7)

Münsterer quotes the poem 'Utterances of a martyr' as an example of Brecht's rowdy contempt for parental authority and bourgeois hypocrisy (compare p. 19). However, in lines from this poem which Münsterer does not quote, Brecht's mother is made to protest:

*This edition of Brecht's diaries contains miscellaneous autobiographical notes not included in the English edition.

> ... that I'd soon have her under the sod at this rate
> And the day would come when I'd want to claw it up to get
> > her back once more
> But it would be too late by then, and I'd start finding out
> How much she'd done for me. But I should have thought of
> > that before.
> > *(Poems,* p. 16)

Brecht tellingly takes up a phrase from this, both in the first versions of *Baal* and in the painful psalm-lament, 'Song about my mother':

6. Oh why do we not say the important things, it would be so easy, and we are damned because we do not. Easy words they were, pressing against our teeth; they fell out as we laughed, and now they choke us.

7. Now my mother has died, yesterday towards evening, on the First of May. One won't be able to claw her up out again with one's fingernails.

> *(Poems,* p. 41)

Others have recorded their impressions of the Brecht family home after the death of Brecht's mother. In the following passage Arnolt Bronnen gives a third-person account of his own visit to Augsburg in October 1922, when he was most upset to learn that Brecht himself had just left for Berlin. Despite the dissatisfaction he expresses at the stultifying atmosphere, he in fact ended up staying for several days as the guest of Brecht's father.

On top of that he was paralysed by the atmosphere at Bleichstraße. Directly behind the house there was a gloomy pond with blackish water. Filmy bubbles bobbed on the surface; they had inspired the young Brecht to compose poems about drowned corpses. In the dim puritanical household a housekeeper mumbled her responses to the dry and rasping tones of the widower father. The only person who seemed at all alive was Brecht's young brother, a slavish admirer of his senior and, like Bert, in some conflict with paternal authority, which neither of them took very seriously.

> (Arnolt Bronnen, p. 92)

Bronnen's frustration at his constantly botched attempts to meet Brecht may well have coloured his view. In any case,

Brecht's father cannot actually have exerted quite such a stifling and authoritarian influence on his sons. Most accounts suggest a fatherly concern for the well-being of Eugen, at worst an amused disapproval and disappointment. All the evidence indicates that Herr Brecht was quite remarkably liberal in his attitudes. Wedekind, for example, was forbidden reading in most respectable households, but, as Münsterer reports (p. 23), young Bert received a complete edition from his father on his sixteenth birthday. He was permitted considerable freedom in his little apartment in the family home. Even after he had left Augsburg he was allowed to keep to his attic room, and indeed spent many summers there. This paternal support endured for many years. His father even visited him in exile in Skovsbostrand in 1934.

In a dangerous and unsettled political climate father used all his connections to smooth Eugen's path – and that despite his own thoroughly bourgeois convictions. He supported him financially, and there was always a room for him at home, however far he had wandered.   (Walter Brecht, p. 161)

Later Brecht expressed his respect in an 'Ode to my father', which tells of the strength and simplicity of the man (Walter Brecht, pp. 265–6).

One little-known letter from Brecht to his father has survived.* It gives voice to Brecht's helpless confusion after the birth of his illegitimate son Frank in 1918 (see below), and it suggests a relationship rather different from that between most middle-class fathers and sons in the period. Brecht begs his father to consider taking the child into the family home, and ends:

I wanted to write this letter objectively, but now it has become a plea after all. You see, I always had it good in my own childhood, and now, if I cannot help my child myself, I must at least try *everything* I can.

And he signs himself 'Your Eugen' – the name by which he was baptized, rather than with his newly assumed literary identity.

*The letter is in the Augsburg Staats- und Stadtbibliothek by whose kind permission we quote the following extract and that on p. 152 below.

II

Brecht and his Clique

Brecht had an irreverent and sceptical attitude towards figures of authority throughout his life. His relationship with his peers was almost equally problematic. Perhaps it anticipates the sometimes precarious collaborative (and exploitative) associations which were to be characteristic of his later work.

The friendship between the two brothers themselves was turbulent, but perhaps merely as full of rivalries as between any young brothers. In this period at least there was still 'a certain shy and tender brotherly loyalty' (Walter Brecht, p. 201), and Walter quotes the rather sentimental poem, 'The tree of brotherhood', which Brecht dedicated to him.

In many ways Brecht had always been an outsider. He was a sickly child and had spent lengthy periods in various sanatoriums. Walter describes a nervous tick which affected one half of his face; and Paula Banholzer, Brecht's girlfriend for seven years, was often disturbed by his physical frailty. The 'heart tremor which familiarized me with the secrets of metaphysics', which Brecht describes in a letter to Jhering (see p. xxvii), proved to be just one of many messages from a weak heart which was to trouble Brecht throughout these early years. His delicate nature brought him closer to his mother and led to the growing conviction that 'he's quite a different sort of man from us' (compare p. 41).

Speaking of Brecht's attitude to himself and his friends, Walter writes:

So far as Eugen took any interest in us at all, he treated us young ones no differently from his own contemporaries. He gave himself patronising airs, which must have appeared almost comical, although we did not see it like that . . .

In order to rub in his superiority, he would often treat us as complete fools and hopeless idiots. In some ways we acknowledged his superiority, but we did not acknowledge it with any degree of admiration; on the contrary, his superior stance distanced him from us. We recognized that he was different, we even went so far as to sense his genius. Not that we were familiar with the concept of 'genius', but somehow it had worked its way into our consciousness. So Eugen's airs never seemed particularly excessive, unjustified, or in any way ridiculous, rather they seemed an annoyance, alien, odd, even threatening. (Walter Brecht, pp. 209–10)

Brecht also rather enjoyed his status and he liked to cut a dash. A childhood acquaintance from Bleichstraße, Frieda Held, remembers how, after the end of the war, she used to see him almost every day striding along the banks of the town moat opposite his parents' house dressed in a pair of jodhpurs:

When he walked along the Stadtgraben or stood on the bank he would often fold his arms behind his back, or slap his thigh with a riding crop. Sometimes he would lean over the fence at the water's edge and stare dreamily for hours at a time into the murky water. I know it's silly but I used to get quite worked up about his carryings-on in those days – because he was such a queer fish . . .

I remember quite clearly how he stood in front of us girls one day and impressed us all with the Nietzsche quotation: 'When you go to a woman, do not forget to take a whip'. I found it very shocking. But Brecht certainly wasn't short of self-confidence. Even in those days he used tell his friends: 'When I get my first car, you lot will still be riding round on bicycles.' (*Brecht in Augsburg*, pp. 172–3)

It all sounds rather different from the perspective of the loyal disciple Hanns Otto Münsterer. Münsterer concentrates on that remarkable aura which attracted so many people to Brecht throughout his whole life, and which perhaps lies at the core of the celebrated Brecht clique.

Eugen was not exactly gentle in his dealings with his friends. Of course they looked on him as a veritable Messiah, bubbling with wit, intelligence and creative verve. However, there was no doubt that, although he never openly admitted it, he felt a strong bond between himself and his clique. For he was inspired by their enthusiastic support, as well as by their empassioned opposition – all the more since there were some very gifted people amongst these friends.

(Walter Brecht, p. 236)

There was a large and fluctuating group of friends during the Augsburg years and Brecht's university time in Munich. Amongst the best-known are Caspar Neher, Rudolf Hartmann, Otto Müller (who changed his name to Müllereisert at Brecht's behest), Heiner Hagg, Otto Bezold and Georg Pfanzelt. Cas Neher first joined Brecht's class in 1911. He became one of his closest friends, and was to remain a friend and colleague for life, becoming Brecht's most trusted set-designer. Georg Pfanzelt, who lived in Klauckestraße round the corner from the Brechts, was a more ambivalent figure. He made a distinct impression on the young Walter too:

Of medium size and thick-set, he dragged his right leg on account of a club-foot. He had a pale, pointed face and dark hair. He was good at mathematics, above average at drawing, and found school altogether quite easy. He played the piano excellently and used to lay on extravagant romantic improvisations. I had the unpleasant impression that he was always trying to persuade me that he had been singled out by a cruel fate. He was sarcastic, had a biting wit, and was probably the only one of the friends who felt truly at home in vulgarity. (Walter Brecht, p. 238)

These were the friends who used to meet at the town moat, play together in the Lech meadows, go swimming or boating, and then celebrate and talk the night away in Gabler's tavern. But their world centred on Brecht's own attic room.

The room had a sloping ceiling. Beneath it stood Brecht's iron bedstead. Opposite the door was a window which looked out over Bleichstraße. The floor was so strewn with papers that there wasn't an inch of space to sit down or move about. It always looked a mess, as if he had just finished working. But if he wanted to lay his hands on something he would fish it out unhesitatingly from amongst this bewildering deluge of books, newspaper cuttings and manuscripts . . .

In one corner of the room there was a music stand with an open score of *Tristan* and a conductor's baton. Bert told me that after his poetic flights he found it necessary to conduct a little, in order to calm his spirit. It must be said, I never witnessed this practice myself. But the music stand made a deep impression on me. There was a guitar hanging on the bedstead. The walls of the room were completely covered with pictures and drawings of his constantly changing heroes . . . From 1918 onwards Brecht's table was adorned with a skull standing on a fat Bible. I had been educated in St Stephan's in the spirit of the great classics and had, of course, little sympathy for such provocation.

(Johann Harrer in *Brecht in Augsburg*, pp. 110–12)

Such 'provocation' certainly had something to do with Brecht's flamboyant tastes, but also with the desperation of a generation that had seen three years of war. Heiner Hagg recalls the atmosphere of 1917: 'Somehow in that third year of the war so many things seemed to lose their meaning. But we had a powerful urge to live life to the full – and Brecht encouraged us' (*Brecht in Augsburg*, p. 106). His brother likewise records that frantic thirst for experience.

One way and another the clique lived in a unique atmosphere, at a permanent intellectual fever pitch. They were fired by the exuberant stream of Eugen's poems, by his renditions with their jangling accompaniments, by exotic literary finds and rousing quotations, and above all by Eugen's own provocative self-confidence and self-aggrandisement, which at times tipped over into downright school-boy megalomania.   (Walter Brecht, p. 236)

Some of the episodes which Münsterer describes are remembered by others of the band as well. Sometimes their accounts make Brecht seem a more ordinary youth. But it is remarkable how often, even for childhood memories, they confirm the extraordinary charge which Brecht seemed to carry round with him. Xaver Schaller was only loosely associated with the Brecht clique. Like Münsterer, he recalls the recitation in the Ludwigsbau (a grand pavilion and café in the town park) by the venerated actor and theatre director Ernst Ritter von Possart (p. 61) – but he remembers a follow-up too:

One evening the whole gang was out on the town again. I remember Neher and Pfanzelt were there, and of course Brecht was in top form. We ended up in a brothel, the Sieben Hasen in Bäckergasse. We were in full swing. Suddenly one of the ladies jumped up on the table and started singing bawdy songs to storms of applause. I remember one of the choruses in which we all joined with gusto: 'There's hair in tufts upon my tum; perhaps I am an ape.' Of course we were well-oiled by then. Brecht scooped up his guitar and began with Goethe's 'God and the dancing girl' in front of all the assembled guests and girls. Gradually, as Brecht retold the story of the fate of the Indian dancing girl, with his goading rasp of a voice and his peculiar rhythms, a hush fell over the bar – until everyone stood in awed silence listening to him sing. When he finished there were howls of applause, someone spontaneously passed round a hat for the singer, everyone crowded in on him, and he had to begin again.

(Brecht in Augsburg, pp. 156–7)*

The technical skill, or otherwise, of Brecht's singing elicited a wide range of responses, but there was no doubt about the spirit.

Most of his songs began life as texts for the tunes he would make up on his guitar. He didn't sing well, but with an overpowering passion – drunk with his own verses, pictures and figures, in the way others get drunk on wine – and he made his listeners drunk with them too.

(Brecht in Augsburg, p. 107)

One of the favourite opportunities to try out Brecht's songs on a new public were the nocturnal expeditions to serenade the girls beneath their windows. Paula Banholzer remembers:

This was the time when he used to serenade me almost every evening.

He had engaged a couple of friends to help him. Otto Bezold, later to become a Bavarian Minister of State, stood patiently holding a lantern, Brecht played his guitar, and Georg Pfanzelt accompanied him on the violin. Perhaps Bez would have preferred to play an instrument too, but his job was to carry the lantern, so he tried to get even by singing louder than everyone else.

The three of them sang me their latest songs, texts by Brecht himself of course and melodies by Pfanzelt, or sometimes by Brecht too. *(So viel wie eine Liebe*, p. 24)

There were several other girls who were recruited to the gang. Käthe Hupfauer was one of the girls employed at Steinicke's

---

*Later, in Danish exile, Brecht wrote an ironic sonnet (*GW*, vol. 9, p. 611) in response to Goethe's 'God and the dancing-girl'. The 'Mahadöh' of Goethe's opening line, which Münsterer quotes (p. 61), is a name given to Shiva.

bookshop and library. Franziska Pfanzelt, later to marry 'Orge', was another. She recalls some of the other activities of the clique:

Amongst our most regular, though not our most solvent customers were Bert Brecht and his cronies, Otto Bezold, Herr Münsterer and my husband-to-be. The young gents often didn't have any money; and Brecht in particular didn't seem to bother much about money. He was unassuming too. When he came into the shop he used to leaf through several books, or even read them on the spot. I seem to recall that detective novels were his particular favourites, as well as van de Velde.* As a rule he returned the books the very next day and took a fresh supply. His appetite was enormous, often it was difficult to keep him satisfied . . .

After a while we three girls became very good friends with the Brecht-clique and were eventually accepted as members of the gang. We used to go to the theatre together, on outings in the country and to the Plärrer; we would roam in high spirits through the dark streets of the old town, or go boating.   (*Brecht in Augsburg*, pp. 104–5)

The Augsburg Plärrer was one of their favourite haunts. This fair and popular festival was held every year in the spring and autumn. 'There you get to know the world as it really is,' Brecht claimed (*Brecht in Augsburg*, p. 174). Although this was the biggest of the Augsburg fairs, Brecht made a point of going to the smaller local ones around the town as well, and would even travel to Munich for the fairs. Many of his friends have recorded his fascination with what he saw as the exotic fairground life:

It was very strange. He had a special feeling for folk festivals. He liked listening to the stallholders' cries, or sitting watching the shows, or just wandering through the fair for hours on end . . . I never asked him why he was so drawn to these festivals. I also remember that he got on well with several of the stallholders and showmen.   (Paula Banholzer in *So viel wie eine Liebe*, p. 139)

Hanns Otto Münsterer himself also felt drawn to the music, the excitement and the romantic associations of the fair.

I suppose they really lead a dreadful life down at the Plärrer, out-casts, trodden underfoot and brutalized. I love these people, they are

---

*Author of a popular book on sex education.

my brothers. It's wonderful, soaking up the music, and swimming in the din of the nightly shows. I get drunk and sated with the whirling sleazy music, which stirs and excites me. We walked through the fair in a long line, arm in arm.

(diary for 26 April 1919, *Mancher Mann*, p. 174)

The rides were the greatest attraction. However, Paula Banholzer and another of his friends, Max Knoblach, recall the limitations of Brecht's enthusiasm:

The swing-boats had a particular charm for Brecht. He was crazy about them, although he could never really stomach the rocking motion. He always felt sick straight away; he was a bit timid.

Paula continues:

I swung like a mad thing, and Brecht went as white as a sheet. We had to stop before our time was up. He breathed a sigh of relief to set foot on firm ground.

(*Brecht in Augsburg*, p. 176; *So viel wie eine Liebe*, p. 139)

Nevertheless, Brecht still adored the swing-boats, and he wrote several poems about them.

Swing-boats

1. You push your knees forward like a royal whore, as if suspended from your knees. Very big. And crimson death-plunges into the naked sky, and you surge upwards, one moment arse-first, face forward the next. We are stark naked, the wind fumbles through our clothes. Thus were we born.

2. The music never stops. Angels blow panpipes in a round dance so that it almost bursts. You soar into the sky, you soar above the earth, sister air, sister! Brother wind! Time passes but the music never.

3. Eleven o'clock at night and the swings close down, so that the Good Lord can carry on swinging. (*Poems*, p. 39)

Brecht was not the only one to write about the swing-boats. Under his influence, no doubt, the fair became to the friends something of a metaphor for life itself. Amidst the reports of the post-war misery, poverty and cold of the winter of 1921 there is a note in Hanns Otto Münsterer's own diary: 'Life is a swing-boat, but you have to know how to swing' (*Mancher Mann*, p. 165); and

he too wrote of the 'fourth great joy' in a poem entitled
'Philosophical reflections on the swing-boats':

> In September when, with song and cheer,
> the great dark swing-boats bring a rush of wind
> you must push – out into the heavens clear
> with heavy knees, and drunk with cheap absinthe.
>
> . . .
>
> The lanterns flicker and your knees start quaking
> and your hands go groping after light.
> Your very soul is gripped with wondrous shaking,
> and your brow is pearled with cooling sweat.
>
> Just at the end, too full with so much swinging,
> it's then you feel the tow of earth once more,
> through tousled hair and dusk-dark winds are winging –
> down through the radiance of night you pour.
>
> (*Mancher Mann*, p. 83)

Brecht and his friends seem sometimes to have lived their
lives with unmatched intensity. And so the private papers of this
period, Brecht's own diaries and letters, confirm the picture
presented by Münsterer's account. In the Wolfszahn meadow and
at the Plärrer they played out their lives as pirates and adventurers. These were days of swimming in the Lech, climbing trees,
singing under the stars and violet sunsets and 'tumbling into bed
like a ripe fruit, voluptuously' (*Diaries*, p. 11).

On the other hand, this life was also almost immediately
processed as art, as literature, and especially as poetry. All the
while it was becoming the material for such famous poems as 'Of
climbing in trees' or 'Of swimming in lakes and rivers', or for the
scenes of Brecht's first great play, *Baal*. As Brecht wrote to
Caspar Neher at the front, 'I'm studying medicine. The theatres
are playing rubbish. They're waiting . . .' (*Letters*, p. 47, Corpus
Christi, May 1918). Brecht was constantly testing effects and
formulations, self-images and selves, from the poet to the rebel:
'In future I shall produce nothing but flaming mud-pies made of
shit' (*Diaries*, p. 11).

Even much later the environment and experiences of his

youth turn up again. Brecht's *Refugee Conversations*, which he worked on intermittently between 1936 and 1944, are a series of humorous prose dialogues between two refugees from Nazi Germany: the physicist Ziffel and the proletarian Kalle. At one point Ziffel embarks on an autobiography in note form, Kalle responds with some anecdotes from his own youth. Münsterer and others have treated this as Brecht's own thinly veiled autobiography (p. 38, and see also below, p. 133). It is of course a highly selective and fictionalized version of events, but it does give some hint as to how Brecht manipulated his memories. Ziffel's third sheet of autobiographical notes concludes:

The hour of utmost contempt in the lending library. The lady with the glasses. Five pfennigs per book. With breasts. In the public baths, without a towel, just 10 pfennigs. The women's section. Chestnut trees. In the distant south. On the town walls too. In the end the boatman and his barge. God's people. And look after yourself.

KALLE: How on earth do you make that all fit together? Do you just write down whatever comes into your head?

ZIFFEL: Not at all. I organize it. Using the material.

(GW, vol. 14, p. 1411)

III

Girlfriends

That same kind of organization, and fictionalization, occurred in Brecht's accounts of his relationships with women. Paula Banholzer, comparing Brecht's recollections of their relationship with her own, comments that 'fiction and truth were never very far away from one another for Brecht' (*So viel wie eine Liebe*, p. 120–1). He was known – and he carefully propagated an image of himself – as a dangerous bohemian, scourge of the bourgeoisie. Nevertheless, it is a very different side of Brecht which emerges from his early romantic encounters.

Paula Banholzer is the girl who dominates Münsterer's account, but there had been others too. In his first approaches to the opposite sex Brecht demonstrated that extraordinary mixture of arrogance and bashfulness which also fascinated Münsterer. One of his very first obsessions seems to have been for the 'pretty gardener' of Gartenstraße, Therese Ostheimer. Münsterer is a model of discretion in his account of 'this first shy and unrequited passion'. He mentions one lost letter which was intercepted by Therese's father (see p. 70). In fact there was a second too, written in July 1916, but this remained Therese's secret right up until its publication in 1988. After an enormously elaborate and apologetic prologue, Brecht finally begins to introduce himself.

You see me every morning on the way to school. Generally I am accompanied by an insignificant and very blond friend, and indeed I am myself thoroughly insignificant . . .

I will dispense with introductions. At the most one might hope to convey the impression of a mind by catechizing its most familiar thoughts. But mine would not stretch even to four paltry pages. Besides, what would it profit were I to give you names like Shakespeare, Goethe, Verhaeren, Kleist, Van Gogh, Marée,* Bach,

*Brecht presumably means the painter Hans von Marées (1837–87) who was rediscovered at the beginning of the century as a herald of modernity in German art.

Mozart (not Wagner), Hamsun or Strindberg – names which are, I trust, but partially known to you – it would be as sounding brass or a tinkling cymbal (I Corinthians 13, 1–4).

My exterior you already know; and it is not, perhaps, the grandest of façades. But then I have never yet sunk so low as to take pleasure in the notion that I was born only to be decorative. No, I was certainly not created just to prettify the streets.

And if you should now wonder how I come to be telling you all this, then I can only say to you: that I am now determined at last to begin my letter, that is, to tell you what it is I really want to say . . .

Eventually, after progressing scarcely further, he rounds the letter off:

In the meantime we have arrived at the conclusion that you may be spared the letter itself. Its message is to be read between the lines. I do not wish to importune you, that is why I am revealing myself to you only towards the end of term, but later I shall have no opportunity to see you, and the holidays are much too long. So if this letter – which has now swelled up to little more than an over-long preface – is not enough to win an audience, or, dare I hope, your permission to write once more, then it would be some comfort to receive, at the very least, a note from your own hand – rather a brief 'May the Devil take you', rather the brusquest brush-off, than nothing at all.

Sincerely yours, Bert Brecht
(first published in *Sinn und Form*, 40 (1988), 1, pp. 5–7)

Brecht's fascination is borne out in a remarkable document which has only recently come to light. A page of his diary for four days of October 1916 gives a rare insight into this agonized and one-sided romance. Confined to bed during the school term because of repeated heart troubles, he dreams of 'the girl who lives in Gartenstraße and has, above all, quiet eyes, which are beautiful and clever, and in which I am a tiger'; eventually he struggles out to meet her:

[Friday,] 20.10.[19]16
Very early this morning I really did set off up Kreuzstraße. It was raining and there was still a strong wind and my heart was playing up quite dreadfully. But I just had to see my little Ostheimer or her

quiet eyes, for I must have something which I can think about all day and all night. But she didn't come, or perhaps she was already in school. I was annoyed and went home as quickly as possible (i.e. crawling, because of my heart), so that they wouldn't miss me.

His humble and chaste admiration for Therese ('I would just like to talk to her – that is all. She has something wonderfully pure about her') rubs shoulders with his usual extravagant self-images:

I am bad, and have sat around in seedy taverns, in fairground waggons, and with soldiers, and I know smutty songs and despise everyone a little because they are so degenerate – but for the children, whom I revere.   *(Sinn und Form,* 38 (1986), 6, pp. 1133–4)

One of the interesting things about this document, which has lain secretly in Münsterer's papers for so long, is Münsterer's own comment about it on an accompanying sheet. He describes it as 'probably an invention', expressly written up by Brecht and calculated to impress Therese. Nevertheless, it is the only diary extract preserved from these early years.

The year 1916 was, however, also the year of his friendship with Marie Rose Aman. With her he had rather more success. She remembers her first impressions of the well-mannered grammar school boy with the 'beady eyes'. Rumours had been circulating about him however – that he had burnt the Bible and the Catechism – and she had a great deal of trouble at school and at home on account of her liaison with such a disreputable young man. She also remembers the pleasures of the acquaintance:

One day, by the boat-hire on the town moat, I received from Eugen, quite suddenly, my first kiss. I was so shocked and upset that I pushed him away. I tried to apologize and explained that I had been frightened because I was not certain whether a kiss would have consequences. Whereupon Brecht said: 'My dear child, you must go to your mother and be told the facts of life. That is not for me to do.'
                                            (Brecht in Augsburg, p. 92)

According to her own account, Brecht promised Marie Rose seven children (compare below, p. 169), in addition to a yearly hat. In the event things soon cooled. By December 1917 Brecht was venting his disappointment and schoolboy pique in a letter to

Neher, claiming that all along Marie Rose had been his own creation: in reality she was ugly.

Brecht himself of course was far from pretty. His own poetry and his contemporaries' accounts testify to that. He was short, with sticking out ears and a rather ratty face, dreadful teeth, and staring eyes – or, sometimes, his unflattering glasses. Besides, he showed no interest in fashionable attire and was known for his shabbiness. Paula Banholzer recalls him promising her, 'I shall dress you like a queen. You will go dressed in silk – so that I can wear what I like' (*So viel wie eine Liebe*, p. 141). And yet he does appear to have exercised a peculiar charm over several of the women he met, both as a young man and in later life. All his girlfriends have commented on his good manners. Paula remembers, for example, how Brecht would kiss her hand every time they met, and is emphatic that the coarse language and vulgar sexuality of *Baal* were confined to his writing and had nothing to do with the gallant and gentle student whom she knew.

The pseudo-autobiographical *Refugee Conversations* offer us an entirely different picture. There are more hints at various affairs and conquests, all conflated and exaggerated. The result is a glorious fabrication, but none the less there are elements which remain identifiably Brecht's. There is, for example, the courtship of Paula Banholzer – although the details owe far more to an adolescent fascination with sex than to the facts (compare pp. 35 6).

ZIFFEL: . . . I was seventeen and I had a girlfriend, a schoolgirl from St Ursula's. She was fifteen but very mature. We went skating arm in arm. But after a while that wasn't enough, I noticed that she loved me, she used to pant so when I kissed her on the way home. I called on a friend for advice, and it was clear to us that something had to happen, but he said it wasn't so easy, if you didn't know your way about the most embarrassing things could happen, and once there was a couple who just couldn't prise themselves apart at all, you sometimes see it happen to dogs, then they throw a bucket of water over them, that separates them. But these two, they had to fetch them away in an ambulance, and you can imagine their embarrassment. Don't laugh, I took the problem very seriously. I went to a prostitute and acquired the necessary know-how.

KALLE: Now that's what I call a sense of responsibility.

(GW, vol. 14, pp. 1414–15).

In Augsburg at the time there were the usual school-playground stories of a society lady who had suffered a vaginal cramp while cavorting outdoors with her lover. According to the stories they had to be separated in hospital. The story of the dogs crops up again in Brecht's diaries of the period. As for the visit to the prostitute, see below (p. 137).

Paula Banholzer (Paul Bittersweet or Bi) became Brecht's first great love. She was fifteen when he first encountered her, the daughter of a respected doctor. The two of them passed each other daily on their way to school. Brecht managed to secure an introduction through Otto Müllereisert, himself an admirer of Paula, then promptly commanded him to keep well away from her. There followed a period of five months during which he persistently pursued her, ambushing her on the way to and from school and all her classes, using all his friends and all his cunning to beg a meeting. Eventually his efforts paid off.

The seasons passed and the arrival of winter brought a unique opportunity: ice-skating. We were allowed to skate in pairs; at last we could enjoy ourselves with the grammar-school boys on the ice, without fear of our teachers' rebukes.

Neither the intricacies of skating nor the cold could dissuade the unathletic Brecht from pursuing me onto the ice. Without more ado Brecht learned how to skate and at the same time dreamt up a trick to save himself the entrance fee.   (*So viel wie eine Liebe*, pp. 18–19)

By the time that Paula had fallen under Brecht's spell, things had become rather more difficult for the young couple. Her parents were steadfastly opposed to the courtship. At one point, when Brecht had been forbidden to enter the house and Paula forbidden to leave it, Brecht, as Münsterer also remembers (p. 36), thought up a novel solution. Paula recalls:

He took off his coat, spread it out on the pavement and smoothed it carefully. Then he laid himself down on his coat, folded his arms behind his head, grinned from ear to ear, and thought it wonderful to see nothing but the blue sky and me. As for the people who had to walk round him shaking their heads or muttering in astonishment, he completely ignored them. (*So viel wie eine Liebe*, p. 26)

He was entranced and confused by her, for him she was 'wonderfully soft and spring-like, shy and dangerous' (*Letters*, p. 36). He wrote to Neher for encouragement, and to Paula herself in romantic exuberance. Both correspondences are tinged with his by now habitual irony. These letters, many of which are now available in English, contain some of the most fascinating expressions of Brecht's youthful attitudes.

Brecht was also extraordinarily jealous. Apart from his summary dismissal of Müllereisert, and a mocking rhyme delivered to Heiner Hagg who briefly, and unwittingly, challenged his position, there were several other occasions when he found it necessary to demonstrate who was in charge. Paula recalls five.

Without the slightest hesitation, he immediately summoned his supposed rival to present himself in his attic and bombarded him with pompous rhetoric, until his poor adversary was completely cowed. With determined control, he would let his voice sink to a whisper then rise to a climactic crescendo, as he rattled through his piece. As if in passing he would mention that I was a poor young thing and that nobody except for him could ever be in a position to offer me what I deserved, that only he had the strength to give me what was rightfully mine. (*So viel wie eine Liebe*, p. 40)

His flights of rhetoric, or perhaps his paranoia, sometimes even led him to blacken Paula's character in order to put off potential suitors, while she herself sat patiently in the corner of the room. He was quite systematic, however:

Whenever he was unable to watch over me himself, he would simply get a reliable friend to keep an eye on me. Then he would receive a detailed report. If someone spoke to me, or if I met someone and exchanged a few words on the street, then his name, or a brief description, was noted down. The name stayed on Brecht's list until – after the habitual harangue in his room – he was satisfied he could delete it. (*So viel wie eine Liebe*, pp. 41–2)

It was a facet of his character still in evidence in his relationship with Marianne Zoff, who became his wife in 1922.

He was extremely jealous and used to employ a few of his friendly
slaves to spy on me. However much he tried to make out he was a
scourge of the bourgeoisie, in this respect he was bourgeois through
and through.   (*So viel wie eine Liebe*, p. 162)

Again, it is Brecht's letters to Neher which offer an illuminat-
ing insight into Brecht's stylized perception of the first important
'affair' with Paula Banholzer. In mid-June, after announcing 'the
most tremendous things are happening', he itemizes first his completion of *Baal*, then continues excitedly that Bi seems now to
want 'it'. These events, and even these formulations, are closely
echoed in the early versions of *Baal*. By the beginning of July his
excitement has given way to triumph – mixed with worry: 'The
ice-cream shop! Chinese lanterns! Bittersweet! (She's all mine
now. Cas, what shall I do if 'it' has consequences? Christ! . . .)'
(*Letters*, pp. 49–50).

For Paula too, the summer of 1918 consisted of a heady
succession of stolen moments with Brecht. Her memories offer a
quite different version of the affair, marked by a nostalgic and
tender simplicity quite at odds with the brash self-consciousness
of the young writer. Paula had been in the country for two days.
Aided and abetted by Bezold, she managed to slip over to Munich
for an illicit visit to Brecht instead of coming straight home to her
parents.

I was frightened to be spending a night alone in a hotel. It was, after
all, my first real adventure. You can imagine how happy I was when
Brecht told me that he had also taken a room for the night and – what
a coincidence! – that he had managed to get the one right next door to
mine . . .
   The hotel room wasn't exactly very cosy. So Brecht – from whom I
had come to expect unusual ideas and actions – suggested that we
should get into bed together, although he emphasized that he only
wanted to lie down next to me – nothing else. Another one of those
crazy ideas of his which you shouldn't take seriously, I thought to
myself.   (*So viel wie eine Liebe*, p. 35)

When Brecht realized that Paula had no experience, he was, it
seems, once more his most gentle and charming self.

When I finally told him, he understood at once. He made no more attempts to seduce me but took me in his arms and explained everything to me. For the rest of the night we talked about nothing else, and Brecht told me all the facts with the greatest sympathy. There was no question of sleeping. Our conversation lasted until morning.

(So viel wie eine Liebe, p. 36)

The next day they walked through the streets of Munich deliriously happy:

We walked over to the Augustiner beer cellar in Arnulfstraße, joking, laughing, and behaving like young lovers do – for all the world to see ... After lunch I ordered a blueberry pudding without thinking of the 'consequences'. Brecht didn't complain. He just cackled with laughter whenever I opened my blue-stained mouth ... At the Mariensäule he suddenly gave me an impulsive kiss in front of everyone. We were happy, and I didn't care at all when people stopped in their tracks to stare at us. *(So viel wie eine Liebe,* p. 37)

That afternoon they slept together for the first time:

I was lying there, half asleep, when Brecht suddenly fell on me in the truest sense of the word, and very clumsily at that.

Brecht was twenty-one years old, and until then – as he assured me afterwards – he had never slept with a woman. I am sure he was telling the truth; otherwise he would never have made such a fuss.

He told me that his friends had advised him to go to a brothel to find out how it was done. He impressed on me that he simply didn't feel he could do such a thing, and that if he had done it he would never have felt able to touch me again.

(So viel wie eine Liebe, pp. 37–8 and 122)

IV

The War

The 1914–18 war, even for those like Brecht who were not very directly involved, was of enormous importance for this whole generation. During Brecht's last years in school, and briefly thereafter, it is a constant nagging presence. Even Brecht's teenage sexual adventures, that he had 'lost' Marie Rose Aman, for example, could appear 'immaterial in view of the World War', as he wrote to Neher in 1917 (*Letters*, p. 32). Neher himself had been at the front as a volunteer since 1915.

Brecht's immediate response to the outbreak of war was to join in the wave of popular enthusiasm. Even many of the most liberal of intellectuals had been swept up in the nationalist frenzy. How should a young schoolboy resist? Brecht dashed off patriotic poems and 'Kriegsbriefe' ('War Letters') for the local newspapers:

Battalion upon battalion is marching off, through Königsplatz and Schrannenstraße down to the station. The cheering crowds mill and jostle round them; and they march on, with firm and steady stride, off to join the great war. The people have brought flowers to the barracks, and now the soldiers' helmets and rifles are all bedecked with blossoms. Beneath the flowery helmets their eyes burn bright in glowing faces.

Not a single one of those who are marching does so other than gladly . . .
(*München-Augsburger Abendzeitung*, 14 August 1914;

Brecht in Augsburg, p. 229)

Walter Brecht has described the same scene, 'Flowers were tossed through the air, and with laughing faces we wished the soldiers good fortune'. Of his brother he comments:

It was with a glowing enthusiasm, born no doubt of the greatness of the occasion, that he greeted the war. He wrote the texts for postcards for the war effort, and one of his friends, Fritz Gehweyer, provided allegorical drawings for them.

(Walter Brecht, pp. 218 and 217)

All the same, there is, quite early on, a shift from such unadulterated enthusiasm towards a growing awareness of the pain and suffering involved in war, and thence to a criticism and even outright condemnation of the conflict. Münsterer himself quotes the very early 'Modern legend' and 'The fields of Belgium' (pp. 39–40), which were among several poems Brecht published in the literary pages of local newspapers (*Augsburger Neueste Nachrichten*, December 1914 and July 1915). He also refers to the rather later 'Mothers of the missing', which was probably already too outspoken in its grief to be published (p. 40).

Finally in this context, there is the school-essay Brecht wrote in 1916 on the subject of the famous line from Horace, 'Dulce et decorum est pro patria mori'. His schoolfriend Otto Müllereisert recalls Brecht's argument:

The saying, that it is sweet and fitting to die for the fatherland, can only be understood as propaganda. To depart this life must always be hard, whether in bed or in battle, and surely all the more so for young men in the very blossom of their years. Only simpletons could be so vain as to speak of an easy step through that dark gate – and even then only so long as they think themselves still far removed from their final hour. When the bogeyman does come to fetch them, then they'll take their shields upon their backs and run for it, just like the bloated imperial jester at Philippi, who thought up this adage.

(*Brecht in Augsburg*, pp. 86–7)

Given the climate and the authoritarian educational methods of the time, it is hardly surprising that this piece should have provoked a scandal. Besides, young Eugen was probably at least as interested in the provocative potential of his essay as he was in its honesty. Another pupil (Walter Groos) remembers the episode:

Brecht sat right at the back on the left of the classroom. He hung his head in shame and listened as the deputy headmaster scolded him; he looked small and pathetic, as any guilty schoolboy should. Dr Gebhard bellowed in his rage, how could anyone who thought he was a poet dare to challenge Horace? It would not be the first time the school had had to expel a writer! We all knew that he was referring to Ludwig Ganghofer who had been expelled from the grammar school in 1871/72.   (*Brecht in Augsburg*, pp. 88–90)

So it was that Brecht was very nearly expelled from school. The comparison with Ganghofer (compare p. 19) may have been small comfort. In the end another teacher and neighbour of the Brechts, Father Romuald Sauer, was able to insist that the essay was the product of a mind 'distressed by the war' (*Brecht in Augsburg*, p. 90), and Brecht's punishment was commuted. Brecht remained fascinated and disturbed by the dangers and horrors of battle. He wrote much about the pity of war, and his correspondence with Neher, who was at the front, returns time and again to the blunt reality of death.

The time was approaching when it looked as if he would himself be called upon to serve. The military authorities inspected his case in January 1918. Notwithstanding his own patriotism, Brecht's father twice intervened with requests that his son's conscription be postponed. The first request was granted. But then came the second muster.

Brecht went to some lengths to circumvent the call-up. Münsterer is not alone in his claim that even Brecht's choice of subject when he went to university in October 1917 was motivated largely by a desire to avoid active service (p. 18). Others disagree: Hedda Kuhn has suggested that he studied medicine because he wanted to be able to look after his sick mother; Paula Banholzer believes that it was a move designed, in vain, to impress her father, himself a doctor. But Paula can tell of another strategy: how he drank black coffee before the army medical inspection, 'in order to overload his weak heart and so be passed over' (*So viel wie eine Liebe*, p. 130). Of course it did not work.

Whatever the truth of these tales, and despite all his efforts, from mid-August onwards the threat of military service was very real. But for Brecht, as Heiner Hagg remembers, it was 'perfectly clear that he intended to survive the war' (*Brecht in Augsburg*, p. 137). There were endless arguments amongst the friends about the war. Brecht's attitude must have been judged dishonourable by many; indeed such differences appear to have contributed to the break-up of the gang. Evidently Münsterer, although an officer's son, did not swerve in his admiration for Brecht. Rudolf Prestel, on the other hand – a volunteer who lost a leg in battle in 1917 and earned the Iron Cross – was not inclined to forgive Brecht his 'cowardly behaviour' (*Brecht in Augsburg*, p. 143).

There were arguments at home too, but Brecht's father seems genuinely to have wanted to spare his young sons the rigours and horrors of the fighting. On the other hand, perhaps he really did think that Eugen was unfit for service; Walter had already been called up in June, and in September his company received the order to the front.

Something strange happened to papa. He just couldn't understand it. He was so upset to see me being mobilized that he burst into a flood of angry recriminations. He, patriotic as he was, thought it shameful that children, as he ranted, that children be sent to the front, with little, or with next-to-no military training whatsoever. In his pain and shock he had completely forgotten his uncompromising love of the fatherland. I understood the sorrow he was feeling, and did not hold it against him.

Eugen and I didn't talk much that evening. He left me alone with mother and father. All the same, the next day there he was, at father's side, amongst the crowds who had gathered to see us off on the train. (Walter Brecht, pp. 285–6)

Walter has described the conditions, the fear and deprivation, which awaited this last wave of infantry recruits. At the front in Belgium in the autumn of 1918 they seem to have been at least as much plagued by sickness and infestation as by the enemy. Eugen wrote to him in October:

Dear Walter,

Thank you for your letter, which much oppressed me. Although I am certain that the war will soon be at an end, I am not so sure that you will be able to stand the suffering much longer. Thank you for telling the truth. There is a wrath in your letter, as powerful as a Greek tragedy; but the thing I find most shattering is exactly what keeps you going (I suppose): the relentless defence of an idea in conditions of extreme misery. I don't think you will die; and you'll choke back the 'flu, just like everything else, and be the stronger for it . . . Here everything is just waiting for peace. These are sunny autumn days, the chestnuts in the avenue are a reddish brown, like gold, and the mornings over the syphilis barracks are clear and light with a trembling brightness in the trees. I am a clerk in the Holl School, with the v.d. patients. Sometimes I get to the theatre, but there's not much going on. Mama seems to be a bit better, she comes and sits in the living room from time to time, it's peaceful here and there's no risk of influenza in the house. I am very much alone, Neher has gone again, and I just sometimes go for a walk under the trees with Bittersweet.

                                                      (Walter Brecht, pp. 361–2)

In a letter to Neher in May 1918 Brecht had reflected on the relative merits of service as 'artilleryman' or 'medical orderly'. In September the decision was taken out of his hands. A brief handwritten note to Hedda Kuhn records his reaction:

Hedda Kuhn, stud. med., Frauenlobstraße 2/0. Please give the ticket to my friend Seitz. I cannot come. My funeral is on Tuesday. Bert Brecht.   (*Brecht in Augsburg*, p. 139)

In the event, Eugen Berthold Brecht served as a military medical orderly at the reserve hospital in the grounds of the Elias Holl School in Augsburg from 1 October 1918 to 9 January 1919. His duties were in Ward D, which was primarily concerned with sexually transmitted diseases. He seems indeed, as Münsterer reports (pp. 54–5), to have had a pretty easy time of it. Heiner Hagg has recorded his astonishment at Brecht's appearance as a soldier:

I often saw him wandering around with his hands buried deep in his trouser pockets – that's how he held his trousers up. He wore yellow shoes and was often without a jacket, just a pullover, usually nothing on his head, and sometimes he had a sort of riding whip in his hand. Of course he never had a sword-belt, he was altogether more of a civilian than a soldier. I often wondered how he had the guts to show himself in public in such an impossible get-up.

                                                      (*Brecht in Augsburg*, p. 140)

V

Diaries of the Revolution

By the autumn of 1918 the war was clearly lost. Within a month of Brecht's conscription there had been extensive mutinies in the fleet. But people had been kept in such ignorance that there was widespread shock at the suggestion of an armistice. In November a revolution was proclaimed in both Berlin and Munich. Kurt Eisner was made chairman of a workers' and soldiers' council (or 'soviet') and the provisional premier of Bavaria. The revolution spread – rather more peacefully – to Augsburg; and the red flag was raised above the town-hall.

The events which followed, along with the war, left their mark on the intellectual and political growth of the young Brecht and of his friends. For years to come German political life was centrally concerned with the writing and rewriting of 1918/19: as collapse ('Zusammenbruch'), 'stab-in-the-back' ('Dolchstoß'), or revolution.

Again, Brecht himself was not much involved, but he could scarcely fail to be moved by the excitement of political developments. On 9 November Kaiser Wilhelm II abdicated, and in Berlin there were mass demonstrations and a general strike. The 'German Republic' was formally proclaimed by the Social Democrat deputy Philipp Scheidemann. Within days the leader of the Spartacus league, Karl Liebknecht, had proclaimed a rival 'Free Socialist Republic', and the struggle for the new Germany had begun.*

*During the war the left wing of the Social Democrats had split off to form the Independent Social Democrats (USPD). Within the Independents there was a radical (communist) group led by Rosa Luxemburg and Karl Liebknecht, the 'Spartakusbund'. The German Communist Party was founded in December 1918, but did not come to prominence until a few years later. Until 1932 the Social Democrats remained the largest single party in the parliament of the Weimar Republic. The important non-socialist ('bourgeois') parties in the early

Brecht was voted on to one of the soldiers' councils, but presumably more because of his well-known anti-authoritarian attitudes than because of any political commitment. There is no sign that he took any particular interest at this stage (see below, p. 149). Unfortunately there are few surviving letters and no diaries from these months. Others of the group, however, took care to record their impressions. The little of Hanns Otto Münsterer's diaries that has been published makes fascinating reading. On 8 November itself he comments that 'there is no time now to write a diary'. But here he observes in some detail how the disturbances continued into the New Year:

9 January 1919

On all the market-places and squares of Augsburg they are burning the handbills of the People's Party.* It's a pretty spectacle, but the Revolution is turning into a carnival . . . They've stormed the office of the *Neue Zeitung*. A meeting of between three and five thousand supporters of the bourgeois parties was broken up by twenty troublemakers. In the Ludwigsbau they are throwing chairs and beer jugs all over the place. They cluster at the rails of the gallery, so as to spit down on the speaker's bald head.

16 January 1919

Brecht came round. In the evening we went out to political meetings. First of all to Dr Dirr. The Centre Party handed out pictures of saints, with the message: 'Your forefathers, the early Christians, shed their blood for their faith. You only have to cast your votes in the ballot box.' When it got boring we went on to the Independents.

A little later on we can see how closely these political developments were associated in the mind of the schoolboy with events in the family, or in school.

years were (from right to left): the Catholic Centre Party, the right-liberal Deutsche Volkspartei ('German People's Party'), and the Democrats (DDP), along with their various smaller and regional allies. The general leftward reorientation in 1919/20 was to an extent balanced by the emergence of smaller proto-fascist groupings.

*i.e. the Bavarian Peoples' Party (BVP), which enjoyed considerable support in Bavaria. In political terms it was close to the Centre Party but was outspokenly regionalist.

31 January 1919

. . . There was a meeting of the School Council which we'd set up. I realize now that there's nothing to be done with these people. My Wedekind talk has been banned, Büchner and Villon too. I've suggested Rimbaud or a study of sanitation in Japan.

1 February 1919

I spoke as vice-chairman in the school assembly, to the horror of the teachers who were there. I was interrupted and not allowed to go on. No one spoke up for me.

3 February 1919

I'm feverish. The soul is man's inflamed appendix.

Münsterer was in fact quite ill that winter, and worn down by the bewildering confusion of events in public life and in his private affairs. On the one hand he was being threatened with expulsion by the school authorities (see below, p. 158); on the other hand the family, like many officers' families after the war, was experiencing acute financial difficulties and uncertainty over whether it would be possible for Hanns Otto to go to university. He mentions the thought of suicide in one entry in January. On 23 February 1919 he continues:

Eisner murdered. The news broke at eleven o'clock at Königsplatz. A couple of the vultures paraded the telegram in glee. The teachers' faces were transfigured with unconcealed rapture . . . I swallowed my rage . . .

The day's momentous events continue later:

All the newspaper offices were wrecked. Landauer's department store was looted. A woman took off her clothes in a shop window and slipped on a dress from one of the mannequins. A milliner's shop and a delicatessen were demolished. They left the books alone.

The Bishop's palace suffered the rowdiest assault. The prelate trembled behind his papered door. They hacked it down. Blood flowed freely outside the law courts. My friend Bez dragged a body to the doctor on a fire-screen, there were no stretchers. 'We'll burn the whole lot of them,' yelled the mob. The police put up fierce resistance. Then they retreated. There were heaps of files smouldering on the streets. 'I must go back for my brother,' a man gasped out, 'they've done for him.' And another corpse was dragged by . . .

This was the day too on which the town-hall and artillery depot were stormed.

The night was blue. You could see the stars. We pressed forward. We crept right up to the fence. There was a scuffle. 'There's a machine-gun pointing straight at us.' 'Forward!' 'Stop! Watch out!' Silence. They crawl forwards like Red Indians. Silence. Then some of them turn back and beckon. 'But no weapons unless you're over 21!' I had to run home as fast as I could. And I didn't get a rifle.

(Mancher Mann, pp. 166–71)

During the second half of April the revolution was effectively mopped up. In these final entries from Münsterer's diary there is a powerful sense of frustration. For some of the young men it had been as much the failure of a generation conflict as of a social one. Münsterer turns to literature for his adventures.

12 April 1919

My parents won't give me any peace . . . It's now become perfectly clear that the older generation cannot and will not understand young people. I feel completely trapped. I feel only hatred now, that dull, brooding hatred of the captive behind iron bars.

18 April 1919

. . . Brecht expounded at length the advantages of a soviet republic. He's such a good speaker. At one point he said, 'Bolshevism is a sickness which will be overcome, but not before our own downfall.'

19 April 1919

Last night I was reading stories from the *Thousand and One Nights*. The story of Sindbad the Sailor. It's a wonderful, powerful book, hard and cruel, filled with the exotic delights of the oriental seas . . .

20 April 1919

Bursts of gunfire from all sides. In front of our house there are armed men chasing back and forth, a machine-gun barks. The Reds are holding the town-hall. Noon. Augsburg has capitulated. We are under siege. There'll be no Plärrer this year.

(Mancher Mann, p. 173)

Walter Brecht takes up the story:

On Easter Sunday, 20 April, after the last resistance at the barricades on the bridge over the Wertach had collapsed, Epp's soldiers moved in and occupied the town.

I didn't see much of Eugen. He was absent from both lunch and supper, which we ate in an oppressive silence; he was probably holed up with his Spartacist friends, getting ready to flee. There was a rumour in Bleichstraße that there had been a shot from his attic window. I didn't hear anything. But later I heard that Eugen, although he was not actively involved, had offered shelter to one of the leading lights of the revolution, Georg Prem.

(Walter Brecht, p. 321)

Georg Prem had been one of the leaders of the Augsburg revolution. In political meetings and around the pubs of Augsburg Brecht had had several encounters with Prem and his wife, Lilli – one of the models for 'Höllenlilli' ('Hell-fire Lilli') in Brecht's *Happy End*. Now the revolutionaries were on the run.

It is true. After the Easter uprising of 1919 in Augsburg I took refuge in Brecht's attic in Bleichstraße and slept there for two nights. Brecht did not sleep in his own bed on those nights, he was a guest elsewhere. (*Brecht in Augsburg*, pp. 167–8)

It has been suggested that this experience of a leader on the run may later have formed the basis for the episode in *The Caucasian Chalk-Circle* where Azdak harbours the fleeing prince.

Caspar Neher's diary for this same period has still not been published – except for a few brief excerpts. The following extracts provide an atmospheric account of a young man's perspective on the last days of the revolution in Bavaria.

Sunday, 20 April

Woken by the roar of cannons. Easter!
You'd scarcely believe it's Easter. The Whites against the Reds. Brother against brother . . .

Easter Monday, 21 April

Spartacus fights on in Oberhausen and Lechhausen, they're holding their ground.

It's wonderful – wonderful, truly wonderful.

Visited Bert, we talked for a long time, we talked about art and politics.

Baal is nearly ready and thrives. It's wonderful.

Baal dances. Baal eats. Baal is transfigured.

Shots on every side. Grenades explode around the houses – and father says I should volunteer for the White Guard.

That's impossible. I can't do that. I can't bring myself to write down everything I heard today about the brutality of the government troops. All for the good of the citizens. Cowardice, stupidity and brutality . . .

Prem put on fresh clothes at Bert's and escaped.

(Brecht in Augsburg, pp. 170–1)

Neher's father was not the only one to suggest that the proper place for a young middle-class gentleman was on the other side of the barricades, with the 'Whites'.

To close ranks and protect the bourgeois world against the Reds' design to replace it with a soviet government of the proletariat seemed to us sons of the bourgeoisie our simple duty.

(Walter Brecht, p. 326)

Walter duly served in Epp's counter-revolutionary 'Freikorps'. However, given Bert's somewhat heedless political attitudes, that did not necessarily mean a breach between the brothers.

I was on duty when Eugen visited me on the night of 8 May. The night before, the sentry had been stabbed, just like that, a civilian had come up to him and asked him for a light. A comrade and I had now been posted to stand watch together. Eugen was visibly impressed with the danger of our situation. The Reds certainly had his total political commitment but they may not have enjoyed his emotional sympathies. Anything dangerous, anything where one might have had to get involved oneself, was not up his street at all.

. . . It was altogether characteristic of him to seek and to proclaim the truth passionately, and no less passionately to give everything which did not suit him a very wide berth.

(Walter Brecht, pp. 327 and 328)

It is relatively easy to establish what everybody else was up to during these months. Brecht's own activities and opinions are a little more difficult to pin down.* He certainly went to political meetings and got to know the Prems – although perhaps as much for the general excitement, and because Lilli Prem was a pretty and spirited woman, as for any conscious political ideals. Ten years later, Brecht wrote about his time with the soldiers' council:

> We all suffered from a lack of political conviction, and I myself from that old inability to get worked up about anything at all. I was given a load of work to do . . . But I was soon able to engineer my dismissal. In short: I was hardly different from the great majority of the other soldiers; of course they had had enough of the war but they were incapable of political thinking. I don't remember it with much pride.
>
> (*GW*, vol. 20, p. 25)

For much of the time he just got on with his life: evading his duties as a medical orderly and being a student in Munich – and writing all the while.

According to Walter Brecht, his brother was actually a member of the Independent Social Democrats, very briefly in February. But Brecht described himself as an 'independent Independent' (*Brecht in Augsburg*, p. 145). Another contemporary, Emmi Lauermann, who was a year or two younger than Brecht and politically very active, has related how she watched him scribbling away at the back of a meeting of the Independents, and even suspected he might be a spy.

> After a bit of verbal sparring we got into conversation, and I was soon persuaded that his interest in our assembly was purely a product of his hunger for knowledge.

Towards the end of January 1919 they met again.

> After a few words of greeting, and the assurance that our political opinions remained the same, I suddenly had an idea. I looked him full in the face for several seconds and said: 'Look, you're on our side aren't you. You should be joining in. We're going to overthrow the government, we want to take over!'
>
> I must have been dazzling him, my eyes aflame with all that youthful idealism, for Brecht tugged that trusty cap of his deep down over his face so that his eyes almost disappeared behind the peak. So I

---

*See also the next section for some explanation.

went on: 'We need you, you can be our delegate for culture.' . . .
Brecht looked me up and down with his dark, beady eyes and his
narrow spectacles. His gaze came to rest on my hand which I held
outstretched before me. After a few moments of silence his face
broke into a broad grin, and with a sudden expansive gesture he
shook my hand and said just one word: 'Done!'

(Brecht in Augsburg, pp. 147–8)

Of course that particular deal could never be honoured; but
perhaps it is fair to say that Brecht's interest in left-wing politics
was stimulated by these various events. All the same, Brecht was
not yet much of a practical politician; for him the outstanding
product of the revolution was the play *Spartacus*, or *Drums in the
Night* as it was later called.

He seems to have avoided direct involvement in the social and
political upheavals in either Bavaria or Berlin. He was in Berlin at
the time of the later right-wing Kapp Putsch in March 1920, but
he slipped away from the strikes and turmoil of the capital on one
of the very last trains. His *Diaries* for September 1920 record
political discussions, but also his own response to the current
economic and political debate: 'I say thanks a lot, and can I have a
car please' (*Diaries*, p. 45).

Within just a few years he would learn to be less dismissive –
but for the time being his writing and his personal situation
interested him far more than politics.

VI

Fatherhood and Marriage

In July 1918 Brecht wrote to Neher about 'a stupid business with little Bittersweet'. They had spent a glorious three days together on the Starnberger See; but now her period was overdue. Brecht was worrying, and waiting for the telegram. His usual banter and bravado were disintegrating, and he confessed, 'I'm very much afraid that you're laughing, but I'm even more afraid that *I won't* be able to laugh' (*Letters*, p. 51).

Brecht's anxiety was justified: Paula was pregnant. Despite his fear that he 'wouldn't know how to cope', he stood by her.

Brecht took his courage in his hands and went to see my father. How daunting that appointment must have been for him. He knew how much my father still despised him!

But he stood his ground, accepted all the blame and emphasized over and over again that he alone was responsible and that I was beyond reproach.

Whether it was a case of insufficient contact between Brecht and my father, or whether these two men had simply no common ground: In any case Brecht's rhetoric had none of its usual conviction, logic or power . . .

Brecht wanted to marry me. My father refused point blank. He said he had always disliked Brecht; now, however, he truly hated him. And he wanted to nurture this hatred and whatever happened never let up.

. . . He would rather put up with a bastard child than permit his daughter to marry a writer.   (*So viel wie eine Liebe*, pp. 43–5)

Some three months into her pregnancy, the young unmarried Paula was quietly shuffled off to Kimratshofen, a village south of Augsburg, so that nothing would be noticed in Augsburg society. Her sister Blanke had been at school with Walburga Frick, who was the midwife in the village, and it was with her parents that Paula spent the lonely time until the birth.

Brecht wrote to her every day, she says, even if sometimes he only had time to send a card with his name on, to show that he was thinking of her. Every month or so, when he could afford it, he visited her, trudging the six hours from Kempten on foot to save the bus fare. She remembers him nourishing himself on dry bread and beet-jam for weeks, in order to send her the precious 4 marks a day that his father gave him. He even contacted Therese Ostheimer, through Pfanzelt, on hearing that she had accidentally discovered Paula's secret, and urged her not to make vicious use of it. Despite everything one knows about Brecht's frequent selfishness, infidelity and cruelty, he seems to have been deeply affected by this, his first great responsibility.

Although my father had made the arrangements to send me away from Augsburg, he was not prepared to give me any financial support. Brecht, who would not have let me down for the world, paid for me to stay at Kimratshofen, and looked after all the expenses. He paid them out of the little university money he had . . . Despite the financial hardship, our idyll remained undisturbed, and there was never any talk of money between us. For him it was simply the only thing to do; it went without saying.

(So viel wie eine Liebe, pp. 49–50)

Frank Banholzer was born on 31 July 1919. The christening was held on 2 August in the local church, with Otto Müllereisert and Caspar Neher as godfathers. The child was named Frank Walter Otto after Wedekind, Brecht's younger brother and Müllereisert. Because Paula's parents would not allow the boy to live with them in Augsburg, Brecht wrote to his father and tried desperately to persuade him to take the child in. His letter, with its loose and broken syntax, reveals his distress.

For however hard I try to get money together, so I can get married and take in the child myself, even if I – I've thought it all through – even if I were to concentrate all my efforts on this, and were to throw everything into it, in the meantime the child would still be in strangers' hands, with no feeling for it, and they would just be making money out of it and would mess everything up.

(Letter in the Augsburg Staats- und Stadtbibliothek)*

*See p. 120.

In the event Frank spent the first three years of his life with paid foster parents in Kimratshofen, before being taken in by a family in Friedberg near Augsburg. Brecht had warned Paula that she should not hope for gifted children, 'for the potential of any one family exhausted itself in a single genius'.* In the beginning he took great interest in young Frank's education. In the long run, however, he had little to do with the child's development. Frank was cared for at various times in his life by Marianne Zoff's parents, by Helene Weigel, and many years later by Müllereisert in Berlin. According to his mother, Frank grew up proud of Brecht; but he was never accepted into the home of Paula's subsequent husband, who hated Brecht and anything to do with him. In November 1943, ten years after his father had fled into antifascist exile, Frank was killed at Porkhov as a German soldier on the Russian front.

The birth of the baby marked a turning-point in the lives of the young couple. It signalled for Brecht an irreversible departure from carefree youth, and for Paula, paradoxically, a greater degree of independence in her life. She arranged to live with an aunt in Munich so that she could be nearer Brecht. Her memoirs tell of the excitement and turmoil of her new life there; but they did not have very many months together. Brecht was already beginning to move in new circles and was desperately ambitious. Soon he was making his first assault on Berlin, out of a mixture of motives – and perhaps as much in the hope of making some money for the two of them as of making a career. This was a city of opportunities and glamour; Brecht wrote letters to Paula crammed with his new impressions, yet at the same time full of fondness and affectionate concern.

In 1922 the first edition of *Drums in the Night* was dedicated to Paula – a dubious privilege perhaps, given the rather sordid nature of relationships between the sexes in that play. But by this time Brecht was also involved with several other women, most significantly perhaps the singer and actress Marianne Zoff, whom he had first met when she had an opera engagement in Augsburg.

---

*See Erich Maiberger (in Bibliography), p. 20.

He came into my dressing room and started making complimentary
noises . . . I was taken aback . . . Firstly at the appearance of this
little matchstick of a man. He wasn't exactly well-groomed, with a
beat-up leather jacket, shapeless old corduroy trousers, and a scruffy
bookie's cap in his hand . . . I couldn't understand why I hadn't
thrown him out yet. I watched him with a certain fascination as one
gawps at an exotic animal in the zoo. I liked his ascetic skull, his thin-
lipped mouth never stopped moving, his dark button eyes burnt
right through you. My eye was caught by his delicate-boned pianist's
fingers. You must be off your head, I thought to myself, as I realized
that I was beginning to like this Swabian bumpkin of an intruder. He
talked and talked and talked . . .   (*So viel wie eine Liebe*, pp. 157–8)

Brecht's side of this relationship is very fully narrated in the
diary notebooks for the years 1920 and 1922. They record the
turmoil of Brecht's various affairs with Marianne Zoff, Hedda
Kuhn and others, and the visits back to Paula Banholzer.

His frequent exhortation – 'Let them flourish, the young
Brechts' – had more 'consequences' than he might have reckoned
with. In March of 1921 Marianne, pregnant now, had moved in
with him, and he wrote of 'living in luxury with the most beautiful woman in Augsburg, writing films'. At the same time,
however, he wondered, 'how long it will be before God's patience
gives out and I'm sitting in the gutter being pissed on by dogs?'
(*Diaries*, p. 80).

In the event, things went wrong very quickly. Marianne
was prevaricating between him and her fiancé, a certain Herr
Recht. Paula seemed to be having an affair with 'a café violinist,
a slimy fellow' (*Diaries*, p. 93). Then, only two months later,
Marianne began haemorrhaging and had an induced abortion.
Brecht, appalled by what he saw as her eternal damnation and a
personal affront to him, railed against her in a vicious diary
entry, and then promptly visited her in hospital to show her
photos of Frank.

Marianne became pregnant again in 1922 and Brecht married
her. He swore to Paula that this was only a marriage for the
child's sake and that he would soon divorce in order to marry her.
He prevaricated endlessly, however, and despite his repeated pos-

sessive attempts to sabotage her own relationships, Paula herself finally married in 1924.

Brecht's subsequent comment to Paula's husband in many ways sums up their long and difficult relationship: 'I treated Bi like a queen, and I tyrannized her, but she never noticed' (*So viel wie eine Liebe*, p. 116). His later associations with his many female collaborators emphasize this dominating and exploitative aspect of Brecht's loves. Marieluise Fleißer, for example, whom Brecht met in Munich at the beginning of the nineteen twenties and whom he encouraged in her own career as a dramatist, comments: 'He was like a vampire, sucking one dry' (*So viel wie eine Liebe*. p. 205). It was at this time also that he met Helene Weigel, who was to go into exile with him and become a life-long companion. And it was she who commented many years later, and perhaps most tellingly, of Brecht's first love: 'Brecht had many women, but it was only ever Bi he loved' (*So viel wie eine Liebe*, p. 123).

VII

The Literary Profession

Brecht had nurtured the unpromising idea of writing as a profession, not just as a pastime, for a long time. After the war, the economic crisis had left the sons of the bourgeoisie unprecedentedly vulnerable: they simply had to turn their minds to earning a living. Moreover, Paula's pregnancy and the birth of Frank in 1919 are events which should not be underestimated in an account of Brecht's early years. They forced on him the urgent realization of personal, social and economic responsibility. So, for various reasons, the years covered by Münsterer's account are the years when Brecht tried to carve out a life for himself as a writer.

His first more public experiments had been contributions to the school magazine, *Die Ernte* (*The Harvest*), which folded in February 1914 after only half a dozen issues. But he had also been submitting short prose pieces and poems to a real newspaper, the *Augsburger Neueste Nachrichten*, since that very same year (see also above, p. 138). The editor of the arts supplement to this local daily, Wilhelm Brüstle, described Brecht as 'a shy, reserved young man who would only say anything after you'd wound him up carefully first' (*Brecht in Augsburg*, p. 66). Much later he was to boast: 'How I discovered Bert Brecht' (*Neue Zeitung*, 27 November 1948). By 1916, and after a good score of publications under the pseudonym Berthold Eugen, Brecht perhaps felt that he had proved himself as a schoolboy 'feuilletonist' and newspaper poet. From now on he generally signed himself 'Bert Brecht', and he began to develop a public literary persona. Writing was by no means any longer just something for the entertainment of his gang and his girlfriends.

Seeking a wider audience for such provocative writing was not without its dangers, however. By no means everybody was as enthusiastic as the close circle of friends; and by no means all women were as impressed with the young self-styled scourge of the bourgeoisie as later legend was to imply. When Brecht got his father's secretaries at the Haindl offices to type up the manuscripts of *Baal*, they were dismayed. One of them, Babette Daigl, recalls:

The director, Herr Brecht, used sometimes to give me his son's manuscripts, which I then typed on the machine and returned. The turns of phrase which occurred over and over in these texts embarrassed me so much that I could often hardly bring myself to type such things. Later on I used to type up the pieces in my own flat. Once young Herr Brecht himself brought me a manuscript which I found morally so repugnant when I read it that I gave it back, untyped, to his father. He just said: 'I can see what you mean', put the papers away and shrugged his shoulders . . .

It was not easy for Herr Brecht to put up with his son's lifestyle. Haindl was a very conservative company. In the firm we thought of young Brecht as the black sheep of the director's family. All the more when he got in with the communist *Volkswille* and started writing articles for them . . .

All in all I had the impression that he somehow had too few positive influences in his childhood.

(*Brecht in Augsburg*, pp. 193–4)

The sorts of influences and inspiration which the young Brecht cultivated came of course from the world of literature; and of the possible contemporary literary models it was certainly Wedekind who impressed him most. Hedda Kuhn remembers:

Those were the days when he promised that we would both, independently, name our first sons Frank, after Wedekind. That was why Brecht's son with Bi was called Frank, and I called my first son Frank as well.   (*Brecht in Augsburg*, p. 160)

Brecht's obituary of Wedekind appeared in the *Neueste Nachrichten* the day before the funeral at which, as Münsterer relates (p. 22), Brecht was an onlooker:

A few weeks ago at the Bonbonnière he sang his songs to guitar accompaniment in a brittle voice, almost monotone, and quite untrained. No singer ever gave me such a shock, such a thrill. It was the man's intense aliveness, the energy, which allowed him to defy sniggering ridicule and proclaim his brazen hymn to humanity, that also gave him this personal magic. He seemed indestructible . . . Like Tolstoy and Strindberg he was one of the great educators of modern Europe. His greatest work was his own personality.

(Brecht on Theatre, pp. 3–4)

The burial itself was, by all accounts, an embarrassing, botched affair. In letters from home Neher received an impression of his friend's more private response to Wedekind's passing, but he also received this poem:

> On Wedekind's Funeral
>
> Baffled, in their black top-hats they stood
> above the carcass: ravens, strutting round.
> And yet (for all their sweat and tears) they could
> not put that fairground showman underground.

Münsterer, who tells of the one 'meeting' which Brecht managed to contrive with Wedekind (p. 24), was also a Wedekind fan, and he too wrote a poem, '. . . conceived at Wedekind's grave' (*Mancher Mann*, p. 15). When, in 1919, he was threatened with expulsion from the Augsburg grammar school, it was partly because he had been seen on the streets during the political upheavals (see above, pp. 144–5), but it was partly simply for reading Strindberg and Wedekind, well-known bogeys of the conservative establishment. The following brief diary-entry of Münsterer's shows, in its naivety, just how these young men went in search of help and encouragement.

10 February 1919

I visited Frau Wedekind and took some flowers. Yellow tulips, I couldn't afford anything better. She wasn't at home. So I went on to Artur Kutscher. His wife was very nice to me and told me to come back that afternoon. He advised me not to try and become a writer. Can it be worth gambling one's life away for the sake of Art? He suggested I should join a big publishing house. I had mislaid the poems which I had wanted to show him.

(Mancher Mann, p. 168)

Professor Artur Kutscher, theatre historian and well-known biographer of Wedekind, lectured at Munich university from 1915.

His seminar was one of the few functions which Brecht attended regularly. It was perhaps hoped that this would offer the young novices yet another opportunity to insinuate themselves with the 'literary profession', for Kutscher moved in literary circles. But the sortie into academia was a failure for Brecht. Münsterer has described the disastrous reception which his manner provoked here (pp. 51–2). Another student, Michael Siegel, has provided the following account:

Of course none of us could even begin to suspect what would later become of Brecht, but even then there was no doubt at all that he was self-willed and obstinate, resolute in his disregard of both praise and criticism, and self-opinionated to the point of arrogance. He was already sporting the famous Brecht-cap, albeit of cloth and not yet leather, and he would peer out from behind his spectacles with a cold, icy, calculating stare. He wore his hair close-cropped and had shaved the hairline in a band about an inch wide across his brow. The fast growing stubble was often visible and seemed somehow to accentuate his hard ascetic image. He barked out his seminar papers in a clearly articulated voice, impassively and never once looked up at his listeners. Applause, laughter, hissing and shuffling all left him unperturbed. One could not fail to notice his Augsburg accent.

I remember hearing his paper about Hanns Johst's *Der Anfang* (*The Beginning*). Several of his formulations have stuck in my mind to this day: 'This work stinks of stage-fright and stale sweat' – 'Hanns Johst's novel amounts to a free emancipation from all the problems of form' – 'Herr Johst's idealism is not so much sky-blue, it's ultra-violet' (he pronounced it 'uldra-fiolett'). He reaped a certain amount of applause, and a great deal of criticism; but compared to the run-of-the-mill academic seminar paper, his was a veritable grenade in our midst. (*Brecht in Augsburg*, pp. 120–1)

That paper was delivered during Brecht's very first seminar, in the winter of 1917. Kutscher relates his own version of the story in his memoirs:

Bert Brecht came running to me, bashful and self-conscious, with a few poems and a Baal play. His own headmaster had already warned me about him, on account of the libellous references to respectable citizens in his newspaper reviews. In his first term he presented an indefensible paper, bolstered with perverse attitudes and adolescent vitriol, the like of which I had never heard before [compare p. 51].

(Artur Kutscher, p. 73)

Of course the theatre professor was not inclined to put up with this upstart student. Hedda Kuhn, who also participated in his seminars, reports how the paper led to a total break with Kutscher, who dubbed Brecht 'a flagellant and a barbarian' (*Brecht in Augsburg*, p. 119). Kutscher never forgave Brecht. The East German critic Ernst Schumacher remembers Kutscher's lectures on 'Drama since Expressionism' during the summer of 1944. There he described Brecht as an 'Asphaltliterat' ('urban scribbler') and 'apocalyptic beast of German literature' (*Neue Deutsche Literatur*, October 1956, and compare p. 51). Later his only revenge was more or less to ignore Brecht.

Perhaps the most important breakthrough to the professional literary world, and at the same time to the world of the theatre, came in October 1919, when Brecht became the regular theatre critic of the *Augsburger Volkswille*, a small regional daily for the Independent Social Democrats, and later for the Communist Party. As Münsterer recalls, Brecht had little patience with the director or the programme of the Augsburg theatre – although they were scarcely worse than in any provincial town. In just his second season he launched a tirade against the director and asked the sarcastic question:

. . . is it not perhaps an artistic achievement of sorts: to prevail triumphant for so many years in that silent, unrelenting struggle against the intelligent spectator – so that, time and time again, the poor wretch is forced to retire from the fray, whimpering quietly, a broken man?

(22 December 1920, in *GW*, vol. 15, p. 36)

But what was really scandalous about Brecht's articles was the outspoken and unthinking way in which he expressed his opinions. The comedy-musical *Alt-Heidelberg* he described as a 'Saustück' ('bloody awful play', in a review of 15 October 1920, *GW*, vol. 15, p. 20); in response the theatre administration temporarily refused to give the *Volkswille* review tickets (see p. 25). In a later piece Fräulein Vera-Maria Eberle, the same

actress who had recited Brecht's poems at the memorial service
for the fallen (see pp. 61–2), came under attack for her 'cold,
academic, prosaic and embarrassingly boring' performance in
Friedrich Hebbel's biblical tragedy *Judith* (12 January 1921, in
GW, vol. 15, p. 38).

Münsterer makes some rather garbled observations about this
last review (p. 31). Only some of Brecht's scorn is directed against
Hebbel and his play, more against the direction and the actors.
Moreover, the great Viennese satirist and dramatist Johann
Nestroy did indeed write a famous parody of *Judith* just a few
years after it had first appeared in 1841. However, Judith's anta-
gonist is of course, in both plays, Holofernes, and not Horribilicribrifax – a quite different vainglorious hero, this time in a
baroque comedy by the seventeenth-century poet and dramatist,
Andreas Gryphius.

By now Brecht's bad behaviour was beginning to have consequences. Firstly, a letter to the *Neue Augsburger Zeitung*:

We feel compelled to report that a few theatre-goers repeatedly disturbed the performance with their quite loutish behaviour. Amongst
these was the critic of the Augsburg USPD organ, the *Volkswille*. His
efforts to demonstrate his 'genius' – which is second only to his youth
– are distinguished by the exceptionally crude tone of his criticisms.
Expressions such as 'Saustück', and the like, trip lightly off the
tongue of this young gentleman, who is himself scarcely – or not yet –
out of his teens, and for whom it might seem more appropriate to
honour the achievements of others. If the readers and the editors of
the *Volkswille* are prepared to put up with such talk that is their own
affair. The spectators at the theatre, however, will not just sit idly by,
while this young man declares his lack of education by laughing
throughout the performance and by disturbing the other theatre-
goers with his conspicuous ill-manners, for example by pushing past
half a dozen other spectators to get out after each scene, and then
repeatedly coming back in after the action had re-started.
(14 January 1921, quoted in *Brecht in Augsburg*, pp. 212–13)

Subsequently, and more significantly, Brecht's review of *Judith*
provoked a charge of libel from the actress Vera-Maria Eberle. A
settlement was reached in April, but Brecht publicly refused to

accept the conditions. It was not until September that the whole affair was settled. By this time Brecht's fines amounted to 250 marks. Nor was this Brecht's only court case.

From these various reviews and articles one can begin to glean some idea of Brecht's literary hates and literary heroes. Gradually a picture emerges of those with whom Brecht wanted to associate himself and his own writing. Wedekind is clearly the dominant figure. Of the more established Expressionists he has praise for Georg Kaiser, for example, but not for Ernst Toller. Generally speaking, he has time for pathos and grandeur, and for the classics, but he has more time for the revolutionary, and for irreverence and parody. He was, after all, already co-writing sketches for that other great parodist, the Munich cabaret artist Karl Valentin. There is a photograph of Brecht from about 1920, to which Münsterer refers (p. 88; plate 4), in which he is apparently playing the clarinet in Valentin's band. Brecht took a small part in a Valentin film too. There is no question but that he learnt a great deal from the master-clown in Munich. In due course an appreciation of Valentin appeared, not in a local newspaper this time, but in the journal of the Munich Kammerspiele, where Brecht described Valentin as 'one of the most forceful cultural phenomena of our time' (*GW*, vol. 15, p. 39).

VIII

Patrons and Critics

Brecht's first real patron and mentor was the older and established historical novelist and dramatist Lion Feuchtwanger. At first Brecht was annoyed at what he considered Feuchtwanger's plagiarism of his own *Spartacus* in *Thomas Wendt* (p. 60). According to Hedda Kuhn he commented, 'He has stolen a motor-car which he cannot drive' (*Brecht in Augsburg*, p. 162). But that mood did not last. One of his very next projects was the collaboration with Feuchtwanger on *Edward II*; they remained lifelong friends and colleagues.

It was not until 1928 that Feuchtwanger wrote up his first impressions of Brecht. From the lofty perspective of a Munich dramaturg in his thirties, the newcomer had evidently appeared quite a bumpkin:

At the turn of the year 1918–1919, soon after the outbreak of the so-called German Revolution, a very young man appeared in my Munich appartment. He was slight, badly shaved, shabbily dressed. He stayed close to the walls, spoke with a Swabian accent, was called Bert Brecht. The play was entitled *Spartacus*.

Most young authors presenting a manuscript point out that they have torn this work from their bleeding hearts: but this young man emphasized that he had written *Spartacus* purely in order to make money . . .

I read this ballad-like play, and I telephoned the shabby man to ask him why he had lied to me: he could not possibly have written this play just because of poverty. The young author became very excited, and shouted at me in a dialect that became almost incomprehensible. He declared that he certainly had written this play solely for the money; but he had another play which was really good, and he would bring me that. He brought it to me: it was called *Baal*, had nothing to do with the god of this name, but proved to be much wilder and chaotic, and a very fine affair. (*Brecht As They Knew Him*, pp. 17–18)

Around the same time Feuchtwanger inserted into his novel,

Success, what Brecht called a 'hideous caricature' (*Letters*, p. 255) of the young writer. This Kaspar Pröckl, to whom Münsterer refers (p. 60), is in essence an image of the older, more politicized Brecht, the Brecht of the Berlin years perhaps. All the same, it contains some of Feuchtwanger's first and most lasting impressions. In this passage Pröckl, a young engineer, is trying to sell his idea for a mass-produced motor-car.

Herr von Reindl meanwhile let his melancholy brown eyes stray with interest over the huge rent on the right shoulder of Pröckl's leather jacket. He remembered having noticed the same rent six months before. Of course the fellow hadn't shaved either. The way he had his hair growing low down on his forehead betrayed a kind of naive coquetry. It was a queer thing that he should be so popular with the women. Kläre Holz the actress, who had both judgement and good taste, had simply been swept off her feet by the fellow. And yet she had noticed what a tatterdemalion he was, and made fun of him. The man literally reeked of sweat, like soldiers on the march. And his aggressive, malicious humour wasn't of the kind to appeal to women, and he smelt unmistakably of revolution. Obviously it must be his vulgar ballads that fascinated them. Whenever he sang them in his roaring voice the women were swept out of themselves. Three or four of them had already mentioned those ballads to Reindl with that suspiciously dewy look in their eyes. He would really like to ask Pröckl to sing him one of them, but the wretch would be sure to put him off. (*Success*, translated by Willa and Edwin Muir, pp. 136–7)

Later Pröckl does indeed sing for him, 'with open effrontery, in a horribly loud shrill voice, pronouncing his words with an unmistakably broad accent' (p. 223), but Reindl still will not build his car.

When Brecht first approached him, Feuchtwanger was already a well-established writer. Even Brecht's own father seems to have had a touching confidence in his judgement – if we are to rely on this anecdote told many years later by his widow, Marta Feuchtwanger, in a letter of 28 May 1968:

Right at the beginning of the decade, perhaps even in 1920 itself, Brecht's father came to Lion and asked whether his son was a gifted enough writer to be able to give up his medical studies. When Lion declared that he was, Brecht's father decided to continue sending his monthly cheques. *(Brecht in Augsburg,* pp. 154–5)

Given Brecht's lack of respect for the literary establishment and given his abrasive manner, he was perhaps fortunate to find friends at all, and doubly so to have such a champion as Feucht-wanger. The young Munich dramaturg, Rudolf Frank, has described his own 'discovery', in 1920, of *Drums in the Night,* in a way which emphasizes the importance of the literary connections which Brecht was beginning to establish:

I was searching. I was looking for something which would express the task and purpose of our theatre, something for the future. And so I was led to consult the well-versed Feuchtwanger. I asked him what modern play he could recommend. I would best like something by an unknown author.

Lion fetched from his study a manuscript which had lain there for some months already. It was badly typed; the original title *Spartacus* was crossed out, above it someone had written *Drums in the Night.* The author called himself Bertolt Brecht and was some twenty years of age. I started reading right there in Feuchtwanger's flat, the sentences raced at me, speaking the language I had heard in the army, in pubs or on the streets, laconic, unsentimental, cold, and yet romantic in its effects, as in its situations. (Rudolf Frank, p. 264)

Later, Frank claims, he discussed with Brecht his inability to construct plots and to create dramatic tension. He credits himself with having provided the stimulus for the formulation of Brecht's 'epic theatre': 'Invent a theory, dear Brecht! So long as you present a theory to the Germans, they'll swallow anything' (Rudolf Frank, p. 266). Brecht, however, had had his own thoughts about theory some years earlier (see Preface, p. x).

In the event, the production of *Drums in the Night* did not get off the ground until 1922, and then under the direction of Otto Falckenberg himself, the director of the Munich Kammerspiele. As Münsterer relates (p. 104), the Berlin critic Herbert Jhering attended the première, and his acclaim (see the following extract) was enthusiastic. At this point in his review Jhering has been talking about the exhausted paralysis which seemed to have settled on German literature since the apocalyptic experiences of the war: 'The worst is not the pain itself, but the loss of feeling when confronted by pain.' He continues:

Anyone who could feel in the air that we must now break out of that barren stagnation, anyone who had already been inspired by Bronnen's creative surge and explosive temperament, must surely be overwhelmed by the utter transformation which a genius can effect with his very first act. The twenty-four-year-old poet Bert Brecht has, over night, changed the face of German literature. Bert Brecht has brought to our age a new voice, a new sound, and a new vision.

(*Berliner Börsen-Courier*, 5 October 1922)*

Jhering was the adjudicator that year for the Kleist Prize, one of the most important German literary awards. Arnolt Bronnen has described (in his *Tage mit Bertolt Brecht*, especially p. 60) how he and Brecht plagued and courted Jhering, and how, eventually, it all resulted in Brecht getting the prize. That meant more premières all over Germany, and the beginnings of a successful career in Berlin.

Jhering was to become a most significant patron, and was to look upon Brecht as one of his own discoveries. His great rival, however, Alfred Kerr, the controversial 'pope' of the theatre of the Weimar Republic, showed little sympathy for the new tearaway dramatist. Kerr reviewed the Berlin première of *Drums in the Night*, just three weeks after that Munich performance.

Despite some signs of talent, and notwithstanding Brecht's natural verve, this play really doesn't stand up. Certainly not as bad as most expressionist dramas, but certainly a good deal worse than the best of them. (All the same not 'expressionist' expressionism, but from the school of Georg Kaiser.) Its construction sometimes like the meaner of the species . . .

Since his *Baal*, I have a certain amount of time for young Brecht, although I wouldn't for one minute want to credit him with talents he plainly doesn't possess. He's not such a stale crust as Kornfeld; not as dull as *tutti quanti* . . . and yet, amongst the expressionists, he is

---

*This and the following newspaper reviews are all reprinted in Monika Wyss (see Bibliography), pp. 8–11 and 4–6, for those of *Drums in the Night*, and pp. 45–8, for those of *Edward II*.

neither so independent of spirit as Toller, nor so luminous. But fresh; but fresh. (*Berliner Tageblatt*, 21 December 1922)

Kerr was one of those who later campaigned against Brecht for plagiarism in *Edward II* and for his use of Klammer's Villon translations in *The Threepenny Opera*. These accusations, which dogged Brecht's early publications (compare p. 33), were amongst the most damaging attacks on the young writer – although they could never be made to stick in a court of law. Of course Brecht's work often involves a montage, a development or a parody of various materials, including literary works; and he did indeed cultivate a 'fundamental laxity in matters of intellectual ownership' (*GW*, vol. 18, p. 100), or, in other words, copyright. None the less, the charges of plagiarism must seem absurd and dated now.

Brecht never learnt to temper the gusto and self-confidence of his literary attacks and judgements either. On the contrary, he developed quite a habit of attacking colleagues, as well as hijacking their ideas. He wrote few formal criticisms in later life, but his essays and poems are peppered with dismissive remarks, especially about literary figures, living and dead. And of course the literary establishment responded. Brecht made enemies, and not infrequently someone would feel moved to take up cudgels against him, on their own behalf or else on behalf of some maligned classic.

Münsterer's own story ends with the première in 1924 of Brecht's adaptation with Feuchtwanger of Marlowe's play, *The Life of Edward II of England*. Again Rudolf Frank is able to shed some light on the circumstances of the production, and on Münsterer's own rather mysterious description (p. 109).

The vast role of Mortimer had been assigned to the gifted Oskar Homolka. Because he was a drinker, I had banned alcohol backstage. But along came Brecht, in the middle of the performance, with a litre of cognac. Mortimer gulped it down, and a quarter of an hour later he rolled onto the stage and babbled his way through the rest of his part. Then on came the portly Mrs Lacis* in her boy's outfit, raised

*Asja Lacis (1891–1979) was a young Latvian who had studied in Moscow. She probably contributed to Brecht's nascent interest in

her index finger at Mortimer, just as Brecht had taught her, and
spoke the only word her whole damned role consisted of, the word:
'Murderer!' But out of her un-German mouth it sounded just like:
'Merde!' There was a roar of laughter, almost like at Valentin's
Christmas tree sketch,* and at the end they all hissed.

(Rudolf Frank, p. 272)

This production occasioned the sort of *succès de scandale*
which was to accompany Brecht throughout his life. Certainly
Hans Braun, the reviewer for the local *Münchner Zeitung*, did not
think much of the evening:

I must admit: this snuffling around in the murkier side of humanity,
this grubbing around and sniffing in the dregs, . . . this literature
written with and for the snout, it is not to my taste nor pleasure . . .

(20 March 1924)

On the other hand, Roda-Roda, for the *Berliner Zeitung*, reported,

The applause was loud and heartfelt; it started right after the second
scene, and returned again and again. At the end a young man who
dared to disagree was given a going over. Peace be with him. Jessner
was in the stalls: so we will be seeing *Edward II* in Berlin soon.†

(*B.-Z. am Mittag*, 22 March 1924)

revolutionary and Soviet cultural politics. She later married the director
Bernhard Reich.
*Karl Valentin had been doing a late show at the Kammerspiele during
the rehearsals of *Edward II*.
†Leopold Jessner (1878–1945) was one of the leading theatre directors of
Expressionism and of the Weimar Republic. He was renowned above all
for the 'Jessner Treppe', a stage steeply tiered as a staircase. In the event
it was Jürgen Fehling who directed the Berlin *Edward*, some six months
after the Munich première.

IX

1922 and Berlin

When Brecht first visited Berlin in February 1920, his future could not have seemed particularly hopeful. On the train he composed his 'Sentimental Song No. 1004', which – with the new title 'Remembering Marie A.' – was to become one of his most famous songs. There is a somewhat adolescent 'old-man' cynicism here, as well as a nostalgic regret at the passing of a carefree youth in Augsburg, all dressed up as a distant memory of one of his first girlfriends. On this occasion he did not stay long.

His second visit, from November 1921, was rather longer and more productive. His diaries give a vivid account. Despite the exhilaration, Brecht was often overtaken by moods of frustration, by the cold Berlin winter and his abject poverty: 'the devil has taken up his winter quarters in me' (*Diaries*, p. 143).

It was at this time that he first met Arnolt Bronnen. Bronnen was another comparative literary novice in Berlin, and in a third-person account he has described his annoyance and disappointment when, arriving at a party, no one took the slightest bit of interest in him:

For someone was singing. That someone had put down his little damp cigar, had cradled his guitar in his lap, pressed it against his sunken stomach, and had begun to intone in a rasping, consonantal voice. It was altogether loud in that room, and only the newcomer [i.e. Bronnen] was silent. This is what he heard:

> . . . It was quite white and moved in very high.
> It may be that the plum trees still are blooming
> That woman's seventh child may now be there
> And yet that cloud had only bloomed for minutes
> When I looked up, it vanished on the air.
>
> [*Poems*, p. 36]

No one took the slightest notice of the newcomer, so that anger, resentment and bitterness had both time and reason to take root and grow. They did not grow, they just blew away, they had never been. The newcomer began to stare at the singer: a 24-year-old man, lean and dry, a bristly wan face with piercing button-eyes, an unruly bush of short dark hair with a double crown sprouting obstinate tufts of straggly hair. The second whirl of hair twisted forwards over his narrow forehead so that wisps fell down across his brow. A pair of cheap wire spectacles dangled loosely from his remarkably delicate ears and hung across his narrow pointed nose. His mouth was peculiarly fine, and seemed to hold the dreams which others hold in their eyes.   (Arnolt Bronnen, pp. 13–14)

So Bronnen was introduced to Brecht, and another friendship was launched. Marianne Zoff, who came to see Brecht in Berlin, saw it all:

'Tiger Cas' and 'Ringmaster Brecht' were inseparable. And then 'Black Panther Bronnen' came along. Cas was jealous of Bronnen's friendship with Brecht. So Brecht thought up a cunning plan: he persuaded them to be friends, so that he could stay in the limelight. Incidentally, Cas used to wear a pair of old-fashioned wire spectacles which were just as dreadful as Brecht's. Purely out of affection, of course. This affection once led to an incident in the small hours one night at Feuchtwanger's place, when Cas, rather the worse for wear, tried to assault Bronnen. With a bottle, I think it was. Dear old Feuchtwanger stepped in at the crucial moment, otherwise there might have been a nasty accident.   (*So viel wie eine Liebe*, p. 168)

In the midst of all this, Brecht was overdoing it. Long days, late nights, too little food and too much alcohol were beginning to take their toll. A few pages after that first encounter in Bronnen's memoir we find Brecht in the Charité hospital with a kidney infection (compare p. 101):

This was something they both recognized from the war years: huge dormitories packed with suffering wretches, foul air, tatty clothing, torn nightshirts and unshaven faces. In one corner Brecht was lying, chuckling away to himself, cocksure and confident: he looked a happy man indeed. Marianne was sitting with him; she had brought him manuscripts, literature and notebooks. A young auxiliary doctor was squatting by his bed. He was so fascinated by his patient that he was at his beck and call at all hours of the day and night. And so it was that Bronnen was robbed of any opportunity to offer him comfort; instead he was comforted himself. Brecht contended that there was nothing more instructive for a young dramatist than to lie in a big hospital ward – better still: amongst the very poorly. He recommended to his visitor that he take his place in the neighbouring bed; he would not want for an illness.   (Arnolt Bronnen, p. 24)

The novelty soon palled, and he found himself 'casting the occasional very cool glance at the shadowy little vulture overhead, the possibility of TB' (*Diaries*, p. 158). On her third day in Berlin Marianne found Bi's letters in Brecht's room. She went down with what Brecht took to be a lung infection. Typically, Brecht had quite overlooked what was actually up with her:

Me? I was in love with him. I gave up my job in Wiesbaden and dashed off to Berlin to sit at his bedside. And then the letters turned up from pretty little Bi in Augsburg, and I poisoned myself. Ah well, as I said: young, in love – and foolish.

(*So viel wie eine Liebe*, p. 167)

Thus 1922, the last year of Münsterer's surviving diary record (Chapter 12), had started inauspiciously for Brecht. After he recovered he concentrated his ambitions and energies on the literary life of Berlin and Munich. Augsburg he had now left behind him, and with it the world which Münsterer knew and in which he knew Brecht. After the Munich production of *Drums in the Night* Brecht and Zoff married. In March 1923 their daughter Hanne was born, but within a year the parents had split up (although they did not divorce until 1928). Marianne Zoff comments on the ultimate cause of the break: 'It was called Helene Weigel, and I found him in bed with her' (*So viel wie eine Liebe*, p. 185).

It was a hectic and, in human terms, costly beginning – even more for those whom Brecht used and abused in these years than for himself. For Brecht the writer, 1922 brought those first premieres and publications for which he had longed – and it ended with the award of the Kleist Prize. Brecht had arrived.

Epilogue

Hanns Otto Münsterer seems always, throughout a packed and successful life, to have looked back with fond sadness to his youth in Augsburg and to his friendship with Bert Brecht, as if this was the time when he might have taken a different path, and become a literary figure in his own right. Several of his poems, even those written many years later, refer to the experiences and the emotions of his Augsburg days: 'Thinking of former loves in summer fields', 'The Lech bridge of an evening', or 'Long ago':

> Long, long ago.
> Just children, that's all we were then.
> But the scented blossoms hung heavy and low.
> Now winter has set in.
>
> But remember then how the moon filled the night
> as we sang in the lanterns' flickering light
> how the spring swelled our hearts with a secret fright.
> Long, long ago.
> And our hearts were so full; they're emptier now.
>
> Do you remember the Wolfszahn meadow
> with the azure sky and no wisp of cloud?
> That tree by the stream where we'd roam,
> it was deep uhunambuhu-tree brown.
> The sky was like a cathedral dome,
> for women and men from the town.
> And our lanterns were stars without end
> and the flowers had faces like friends.
> Of course, we were poets then.
> The war brought blood to the banks of the Lech,
> but my friend was Bert Brecht. –
> It's long, long ago.   (*Mancher Mann*, p. 94)

Unlike Münsterer, Brecht felt little nostalgia for these years. Nevertheless, even after he had adopted Berlin as his home and had largely left the haunts and friendships of his youth behind, he still carried Augsburg with him, both in his affections, and in his strong southern accent. In August 1932, long after he was established in the capital, he bought his first house on the Ammersee, halfway between Augsburg and Munich, in order to keep a foothold in the familiar territory of his youth. After February 1933 everything changed. Brecht was forced into exile 'changing countries oftener than our shoes' (*Poems*, p. 320), and was not to return to Germany for fifteen years. It seemed inevitable that the secure world of the Augsburg years should retreat in the face of the horrors of war. Yet the links were not entirely broken: in 1938/9 he described himself as the 'Augsburger walking with Dante through the Inferno of the Departed' (*GW*, vol. 9, p. 613). Some of his family and old Augsburg friends visited him in Denmark and Sweden. And familiar tastes died hard. An anecdote from his years in the United States relates how he surveyed a choice meal served in his honour with some mistrust, before pushing it aside with the words, 'We don't eat stuff like that in Augsburg' (Müller/Semmer, pp. 3–4, see Bibliography).

With the war raging in Europe Brecht thought back to his hometown and to the devastation that it might be suffering:

Homecoming

My native city, however shall I find her?
Following the swarms of bombers
I come home.
Well, where is she? Where the colossal
Mountains of smoke stand.
That thing there amongst the fires
Is her.

My native city, how will she receive me?
Before me go the bombers. Deadly swarms
Announce my homecoming to you. Conflagrations
Precede your son.   (*Poems*, p. 392)

That poem was written in 1943. On the night of 25 February 1944 Augsburg was bombed, and much of the centre of the town was flattened.

After the war, as soon as communication became possible once more, Brecht wrote to his old friend Georg Pfanzelt in Augsburg: 'Dear George, I don't know what has happened, but I have a feeling that you're still around'; and later:

Otto tells me your house is in ruins, and I imagine that a walk down the Lech will be rather depressing. But now at least there's a possibility of our seeing each other again. Though it's not all that simple from here . . . Cas has written to me from Hamburg. I know that Hartmann is dead . . .

I'm glad the world still has you in it. Regards to your wife.

Your old
b   (*Letters*, pp. 406 and 413)

Brecht's letters are fully of sympathy and offers of concrete help, but they are also full of sad, ironic memories of the Augsburg of his youth: 'I gather from your letter that at least the Lech is still there. So there's still enough left for a third World War' (*Letters*, p. 424).

Brecht returned to Europe in 1947, moving from Switzerland to Berlin (East) in 1949. In September 1949 he paid his only return visit to Augsburg when he went with Ruth Berlau to visit Pfanzelt and to see his parents' grave. There was next-to-no further contact. This last poem was written in 1955, shortly before Brecht's death.

> Difficult Times
>
> Standing at my desk
> Through the window I see the elder tree in my garden
> And recognize something red in it, something black
> And all at once recall the elder
> Of my childhood in Augsburg.
> For several minutes I debate
> Quite seriously whether to go to the table
> And pick up my spectacles, in order to see
> Those black berries again on their tiny red stalks.
>
> (*Poems*, p. 449)

After all that had happened, Brecht was bound to have mixed feelings about Augsburg. The city itself has had, since the war, a notably difficult relationship with its most radical and controversial son. Some ten years after his death, however, the street along the town moat opposite his parents' house, the former Frühlingsstraße, was renamed: Bert-Brecht-Straße.

German originals of Brecht verse in *The Young Brecht*

The following are the original German texts of Brecht's poems as quoted in Hanns Otto Münsterer's memoir (see Editors' and Translators' Note, p. xii) with page reference to their appearance in this volume. The Brecht poems quoted in 'Further Perspectives' are translated from the standard German edition of his works.

5 Als nun kam das vierte Jahr,
   war es ihnen offenbar,
   daß es ein Krieg der Reichen war
   und daß die Reichen den Krieg nur führten,
   damit die Reichen noch reicher würden.

7 Er barg in Augen sanft und schön
   einen wüsten Fluch.
   Ihm hing vom zerfranzten Knopfloch obszön
   eine weiße sanfte Nelke mit einem Leichenruch.

   Weit mehr als hohe Stirnen
   war ihm ein goldenes Haar;
   doch entjungferte er die Dirnen
   nicht unter 15 Jahr.

   Und ging *es*, so ging *er* nicht schief:
   Er hatte bläuliches Blut.
   Er zog vor jedem schönen Baume tief
   seinen (sonderbar schäbigen) Hut.

   Trug stets einen feinen grauen
   Handschuh verflucht elegant:
   Er gab nur Tieren und Frauen
   seine nackte Hand.

15   . . . leise wie eine Zofe
      Cassens Lied mit der *einen* Strophe:
      Wenn doch bald Frieden wär und ich daheim.

19   Ich zum Beispiel spiele Billard in der Bodenkammer
      wo die Wäsche zum Trocknen aufgehängt ist und pißt.
      Meine Mutter sagt jeden Tag: Es ist ein Jammer
      wenn ein erwachsener Mensch so ist

      und so etwas sagt, wo ein anderer Mensch nicht an
                                    so etwas denkt
      bei der Wäsche, das ist schon krankhaft, so was
                              macht ein Pornographist.
      Aber wie mir dieses Blattvordenmundnehmen zum
                              Hals heraushängt!
      Und ich sage zu meiner Mutter: Was kann denn ich
                        dafür, daß die Wäsche so ist!

      Dann sagt sie: So etwas nimmt man nicht in den
                              Mund, nur ein Schwein.
      Dann sage ich: Ich nehme es ja nicht in den Mund . . .

      Dann sollen sie eben nichts von der Wahrheit in
                              dem Katechismus drucken,
      wenn man nicht sagen darf, was ist.

34   Denn nach der Maiandacht,
      da kam die Maiennacht.

35   Teddy sagt, sie kann nun einmal nicht so spröde sein,
      da stecke sie schon lieber so 'nen Kuß noch ein.
      Ja das glaube, wer kann und mag, meine Herrn!
      Schwamm drüber, selig wird jeder gern.

      Teddy sagt vom Intimsein, wenn sie's öffentlich sei,
      da seh es doch jeder und da sei nichts dabei.
      Ja das glaube, wer kann und mag, meine Herrn!
      Schwamm drüber, selig wird jeder gern.

39 Seine Dornenkrone
    nahmen sie ab,
    legten ihn ohne
    die Würde ins Grab.

    Als sie gehetzt und müde
    andern Abends zum Grabe kamen,
    siehe, da blühte
    aus dem Hügel jenes Dornes Samen.

39 In der Nacht noch spät
    sangen die Telegraphendräht'
    von den Toten, die auf dem Schlachtfeld geblieben.
    Siehe, da ward es stille bei Freunden und Feinden.
    Nur die Mütter weinten
    hüben und drüben.

40 Immer um die Maienzeit
    kauft Bert Brecht sich neue Hüte,
    trägt sie heim in einer Düte.

40 Jetzt wachen nur noch Mond und Katz,
    die Mädchen alle schlafen schon,
    da trottet übern Rathausplatz
    Bert Brecht mit seinem Lampion.

41 Wenn ich bei den feinen Leuten sitze
    und erzähle, was noch keiner weiß,
    schauen sie mich so an, daß ich schwitze,
    und man schwitzt nicht in dem feinen Kreis.
    Und dann sehen sie sich an und lachen,
    und sie sagen ganz wie meine Mutter:
    Er ist ein andrer Mensch, er ist ein andrer Mensch,
    er ist ein völlig andrer Mensch als wir.

    Wenn ich einst in Gottes Himmel komme,
    und ich komm hinein, laßt euch nur Zeit,
    sagen alle, Heilige und Fromme:
    Der hat uns gefehlt zur Seligkeit!

und dann sehen sie sich an und lachen,
und sie sagen ganz wie meine Mutter:
Er ist ein andrer Mensch, er ist ein andrer Mensch
er ist ein völlig andrer Mensch als wir.

43 Wir tanzten nie mit mehr Grazie
als über die Gräber noch.
Gott pfeift die schönste Melodie,
stets auf dem letzten Loch.

43 Litje Pu, die Leichenfrau,
macht die Sache ganz genau,
wäscht dir rein die schmutzigen Glieder,
gibt dich rein der Erde wieder.
Sie wäscht dich wie im Mutterleib . . .

44 Die Jungfrau hat geboren.
Sie wiegt ihr keusches Kind.
Der Jüngling ging über die Berge,
wo Ideale sind.

44 schau, schau,
der schönste Ort
im Ludwigsbau
ist der Abort.

46 Mein Herz ist trüb wie die Wolke der Nacht
und heimatlos, oh du!
Die Wolken des Himmels über Feld und Baum,
die wissen nicht wozu?
Sie haben einen weiten Raum.

Mein Herz ist wild wie die Wolke der Nacht
und sehnsuchtsvoll, oh du!
Die will der ganze weite Himmel sein,
und sie weiß nicht wozu?
Die Wolke der Nacht ist mit dem Wind allein.

47 Ob es Gott gibt oder keinen Gott
    kann, so lang es Baal gibt, Baal gleich sein.
    Aber das ist Baal zu ernst zum Spott:
    ob es Wein gibt oder keinen Wein.

49 'Der Baum, den mein Sturm faßt, fühlt seine Wurzeln, und
    wenn er gestorben ist, muß er blühn, es hilft ihm nichts. Freund
    sind dir alle Dinge, wenn du blind bist und sie sind nicht mehr
    da für dich! Aber aller Licht gebe ich in dich und du erleuchtest
    alles! Nun sollst du sterben, denn du hast es verdient: Allzeit
    hast du mir gedient und selbst deine Niederlage war mein
    Triumph.'

    ER: 'Herr, ich weiß, wer du bist, denn es ist schon still worden in
    mir.

    *Tür und Fenster der Stube springen auf, blaue Nacht wird sichtbar,
    eine fern wehende ruhige Musikstimme hebt an.*

    Wie ist das, daß die Nacht anhebt zu singen. Und der Baum
    singt und die Decke und das Gebälk singt auch. Ich bin
    voll Unruhe als gebäre ich eine Welt und bin doch nur ein
    Staubteil, das du trunken gemacht hast, daß es seine Kleinheit
    vergißt aus schwachem Hirn und sich vermißt eine Welt zu
    machen! Aber ich will still sein, denn es hören nicht, die nur
    reden.'

    *Viele Stimmen, immer mehr sich einend, singen eine Messe. – E R
    taumelt mit hoch erhobenen Händen durchs Tor in die Nacht
    hinaus. – Stimmen ohne Worte erfüllen die leere, sich verdunkelnde
    Bühne.*

52 Heilgei sagt, du seist ein alter Knochen,
    aber Heilgei ist auch nicht galant.
    Na, der Orge hat es gleich gerochen,
    wie es wohl um deine Herkunft stand.

    Eine Tante, Hoch! schrie er mit Feuer.
    Seht ihr, daß sie keine Zähne hat,
    aber Kiefer hat sie ungeheuer!
    Seht ihr, dieses Biest war niemals satt!

52   so ein Kind, das sich der Männer wehrte
und sie schließlich himmlisch duldend litt.

53   dessen Lied sich süß wie – Milch ergoß,
der bestrahlt vom Glanz himmlischer Lichter
einen Lampion im Rausch erschoß.

53   Was du warst, jetzt bist du es gewesen.
Übrig bleibt ein warnendes Symbol.

55   Oh, du ahnst nicht, was ich leide,
seh ich eine schöne Frau,
die den Steiß in gelber Seide
schwenkt im Abendhimmelblau.

55   Oh, wie brannten euch der Liebe Flammen,
als ihr jung und voller Feuer wart,
denn es haut der Mensch das Mensch zusammen
und das ist nun einmal seine Art.

55   Oh diese Weiber, Himmelherrgottsakrament!
Arg schon die Liebe, aber ärger noch der Tripper brennt!

58   Litaipcc kann in siebzig Sprachen reden.
Siebzig Teufel der Hölle können ihn nicht versuchen.
Litaipee kann in siebzig Sprachen beten.
In siebzig Sprachen kann Litaipee fluchen.

58   War einst eine junge Nonne
zu Sankt Maria Stern.

58   Es hat ein jeder Stand seine Pflicht.
     Die Musiker machen Radau.
     Der Pfarrer macht ein frommes Gesicht
     und die Ärzte machen k.v.

58   Und den Absinth und fauler Schlamm
     in dieser Straßen Kot ausspie,
     den fraß die Tabes in den breiten Schenkeln
     der Schwestern unsrer lieben Frau Marie.

59   Die roten Fahnen der Revolutionen
     sind längst von den Dächern herabgeweht.

61   Wenn ihr Kot macht, ist's, sagt Baal, gebt acht,
     besser noch, als wenn ihr gar nichts macht.

63   Schwankt dir die Erde, Himmel schwankt auch.
     Schädel mag leer sein, ist Schnaps nur im Bauch.

63   Schwimmst du hinunter, Ratten im Haar,
     der Himmel drüber bleibt wunderbar.

65   Halben Weges zwischen Nacht und Morgen,
     nackt und frierend zwischen dem Gestein,
     unter kalten Himmeln wie verborgen,
     muß der Himmel der Enttäuschten sein.

65   . . . in meinen Jugendja-ahren
     war der Frühling schöner noch als heut.
     Daß die schönen Mädchen schöner wa-aren,
     ist das Letzte, was uns Alte freut.

66   Wie dem auch sei, einmal
     hatte ich sie sehr lieb.

66   Von allen Mädchen, längst schon vergessenen,
      weiß ich, sie waren gut, als ich sie küßte,
      nur von ihr, nur von ihr, die mir die liebste war,
      weiß ich das nicht.

68   Der Frühling sprang durch den Reifen
      des Himmels auf grünen Plan.
      Da kam mit Orgeln und Pfeifen
      der Plärrer bunt heran.

70   In einem Frühling kam an ein Gestade
      ein fremdes Schiff, das blau war wie das Meer
      mit schlaffen Segeln und geschloßner Lade
      und ohne Paß und mutterseelenleer.

      Viel sonnige Tage lag es dort und viele
      sahn es vom Ufer sonnenhell und nah,
      bis es so lang lag, daß die blauen Kiele
      kein Mensch mehr drüben schaukeln sah.

      Nur nachts zuweilen hörten sehr Berauschte
      in seinem Takelwerk fremde Musik
      und dennoch: keiner der erstaunend lauschte,
      und dennoch: keiner, dem der Wind die Segel bauschte,
      nahm Müh und Mut, daß er das Schiff bestieg.

      Es folgte einem fremden Sterne
      zu landen einst an einem Riff –
      denn mit dem Lenz in nebelblauer Ferne
      verschwand das blaue geisterhafte Schiff.

71   [by Münsterer]

      Immer, wenn Frühling ist, schaukeln die Kähne nachts
      zwischen den Wassern, immer, wenn Frühling ist,
      singen die Mädchen, tropft vom Gezweig der Tau
      und von der Mauer rieseln die Blüten.

      Als du ein Jüngling warst, toll von der Maiennacht,
      Weihrauch im Haar noch, trieb es vom Domportal
      fort dich zum Graben. Schaukelnd im Dämmerlicht
      zitternder Ampeln schwankten die Gondeln.

Damals lehntest du scheu, heiß von dem Sang der Nacht
dort an den Stämmen. Tau fiel und Blütenstaub
über die Hand dir, bis sich in wildem Kuß
seliger Glut die Lippen gefunden.

Jahre sind weggeweht. Jetzt steht dein Sohn vielleicht
bei den Kastanien. Oder dein Enkel schon
steuert den Nachen: immer noch grünt der Baum,
immer noch klirrt das Lachen der Mädchen.

So ist die Frühlingsnacht. Wenn du auch tausend Jahr
schläfst in den Gräbern, wenn deinen Namen längst
keiner mehr ausspricht: Ewig singt fort das Lied,
lachen die Mädchen, klatscht vom Gezweig der Tau
durch der Geschlechter endlose Kette.

75 Ihr fragt, wie lange sind sie schon beisammen?
Seit kurzem.
                Und wann werden sie sich trennen?
                                        Bald.
So scheint die Liebe Liebenden ein Halt.

82 Und er watete im Dreck, Dreck, Dreck
doch der Dreck, der ging nicht weg.

82 Heute nacht war Kampf
und der Feind war da, ah Mama.

83 Sie war so glücklich und selig
wie lachenden Himmels Blau,
ihre Freuden waren unzählig,
sie war eine herrliche Frau.

83 Dieser Neger war nicht schön,
auch war er nicht herrisch,
auch war er nicht elegant,
sondern nur der Polizei bekannt.

86 Rom schloß die Tore. Sonst kam keine Änderung.
Alltag und Allnacht. Essen. Schlafen. Zeugen.
Sonst störte keine Änderung die Stadt.

90 Die Tage deiner Bitternisse
sind bald vorüber nun, mein Kind,
wie die der unerhörten Küsse
auch bald vorbeigegangen sind.

Bald wird das Leben nur noch symbolisch,
der Tod sogar verliert den Zweck,
bald ist es soweit, bald wirst du katholisch
und schlummerst sanft im geweihten Dreck.

94 Er war Diener in dem Institute,
mußte stets im kalten Keller sein,
alle Leichen reinigt er vom Blute
und schob sie in einen Ofen rein.

Dieser Ofen strahlte keine Wärme,
sondern Eiseskälte zum Gefriern.
Waren steifgefroren die Gedärme,
konnte man sie mit Genuß seziern.

97 John-I-am-happy schlief in der Seehundsbar
und spielte Poker und Can't,
und als seine Seele verpokert war,
da wurde John Sergeant.

John-I-am-happy,
wer ist deine Mutter, hee?
Es habt ihr schwarzen Schweine
vor Gottes Thron einst keine,
die für euch dort einsteh!
da sagte, rein wie Schnee,
John-I-am-happy, seine
sei die Mama Armee.

100 Jenny, liebste Jenny mein,
wann gehen wir zur Ruh,
da sagt die Jenny, die andern Herrn
die sind ja viel netter als du.

108 Johnny, nimmt deinen Pfriem heraus, wie?
     Johnny spuck nicht in die Jalousie!

     Wahrlich, es gibt nichts Schlimmeres im Himmel und auf
         Erden
     als von einem dieser langhaarigen Wesen geheiratet zu
         werden.

108 An der Saale hellem Strande
     stehen Burgen stolz und hehr,
     doch kein Ritter stößt ins Horne,
     keine Ader schwillt vom Zorne,
     und die Kerker stehen leer.

112 In den finstern zeiten
     wird auch da gesungen werden?
     da wird auch gesungen werden
     von den finstern zeiten.

Select Bibliography

Brecht

English-language readers have at their disposal the ongoing large-scale edition of Brecht's works, with useful notes and annotations, under the overall editorship of John Willett. This edition is used widely in this book (see p. xv, Abbreviations, for details of the individual volumes); in addition to the works listed, twelve volumes of the *Collected Plays* are available, and *Poems & Songs from the Plays* (London, 1990).

The main German edition is *Gesammelte Werke in 20 Bänden*, edited by Suhrkamp Verlag in association with Elisabeth Hauptmann and others (Frankfurt, 1967). A new and fuller *Berliner und Frankfurter Ausgabe*, projected as 30 volumes, began to appear in 1988.

Of further particular relevance to the young Brecht, besides the German editions of the letters and diaries (listed on p. xv) are Brecht's 'Tagebuchaufzeichnungen 1916' and 'Brief an Therese Ostheimer', which appeared respectively in *Sinn und Form*, 38 (1986), no. 6, pp. 1133–5 and 40 (1988), no. 1, pp. 5–7, and *Briefe an Marianne Zoff and Hanne Hiob*, edited by Hanne Hiob (Frankfurt, 1990). Unpublished material is held in various archives and libraries, especially the Bertolt-Brecht Archiv, 125 Chausseestraße, Berlin, the Staats- und Stadtbibliothek Augsburg, and the Bayerisches Staatsarchiv, Munich.

The following is a selection of accounts of the young Brecht on which this book has drawn, or which are mentioned by Münsterer in the text. English publications are asterisked.

Paula Banholzer and others, *So viel wie eine Liebe: Der unbekannte Brecht*, edited by Axel Polder and Willibald Eser (Munich, 1981).

Walter Brecht, *Unser Leben in Augsburg, damals* (Frankfurt, 1984).

Arnolt Bronnen, *Tage mit Bertolt Brecht: Geschichte einer unvollendeten Freundschaft* (Munich, 1960).

Wilhelm Brüstle, 'Wie ich Bert Brecht entdeckte' in *Neue Zeitung* (Munich), 27 November 1948.

Franco Buono, *Bertolt Brecht 1917–22: Jugend, Mythos, Poesie* (Göttingen 1988, originally Bari 1983).

*Lion Feuchtwanger, 'Bertolt Brecht Presented to the British', reprinted in Witt (below).

   Success, translated by Willa and Edwin Muir (London 1930, first published in German in 1928) – a novel with portraits of various contemporaries, including Brecht.

Rudolf Frank, *Spielzeit meines Lebens* (Heidelberg, 1960).

Werner Frisch and K. W. Obermeier, *Brecht in Augsburg: Erinnerungen, Texte, Fotos. Eine Dokumentation* (Berlin and Weimar, 1975; reprinted Frankfurt, 1976).

Willi Haas, *Bert Brecht* (Berlin, 1958).

*Ronald Hayman, *Bertolt Brecht* (London, 1983).

Werner Hecht, *Bertolt Brecht: Sein Leben in Bildern und Texten* (Frankfurt, 1978).

Max Högel, *Bertolt Brecht: Ein Porträt* (Augsburg, 1962), originally in *Lebensbilder aus dem Bayerischen Schwaben*, vol. 8 (Munich, 1961).

Max Hohenester (under the pseudonym 'C. Lischer'), 'Bert Brechts Augsburger Zeit' in *Schwäbische Landeszeitung* (Augsburg), 30 April 1947.

Horst Jesse, *Spaziergang mit Bertolt Brecht durch Augsburg* (Augsburg, 1985).

Artur Kutscher, *Der Theaterprofessor: Ein Leben für die Wissenschaft vom Theater* (Munich, 1960).

Erich Maiberger, 'Brechts Augsburger Jahre', in Otto Knörrich (ed.), *Geschichte des Realgymnasiums Augsburg* (Augsburg, 1964).

Werner Mittenzwei, *Das Leben des Bertolt Brecht* (Berlin and Weimar, 1986).

André Müller and Gerd Semmer (eds), *Geschichten vom Herrn B.: Gesammelte Brecht-Anekdoten* (Frankfurt, 1980).

Carl Pietzcker, *Die Lyrik des jungen Brecht: vom anarchischen Nihilismus zum Marxismus* (Frankfurt, 1974).

   Ich kommandiere mein Herz: Brechts Herzneurose, second edn (Würzburg, 1988).

Dieter Schmidt, *'Baal' und der junge Brecht: Eine textkritische Untersuchung zur Entwicklung des Frühwerks* (Stuttgart, 1966).

Ernst Schumacher, *Die dramatischen Versuche Bertolt Brechts 1918–1933* (Berlin, 1954).
'Er wird bleiben', *Neue Deutsche Literatur*, 4(1956), no.10, pp. 18–28.
and Renate Schumacher, *Leben Brechts in Wort und Bild* (Berlin, 1979).
Klaus Schuhmann, *Der Lyriker Bertolt Brecht 1913–1933* (Berlin, 1964).
*Sergei Tretyakov, 'Bert Brecht', reprinted in Witt (below).
*Klaus Völker, *Bertolt Brecht: A Biography*, translated J. Nowell (London, 1979, originally Munich, 1976).
Albrecht Weber, 'Brechts Verhältnis zu Augsburg', in Willy Schweinberger (ed.), *2000 Jahre Augsburg* (Augsburg, 1984).
*Hubert Witt (ed.), *Brecht As They Knew Him*, translated by John Peet (London 1975, originally in a longer German version, Leipzig, 1964).
Monika Wyss, *Brecht in der Kritik: Rezensionen aller Brecht-Uraufführungen* (Munich, 1977).

Münsterer

Hanns Otto Münsterer was the author of several works besides *The Young Brecht*. There are several short pieces and lectures about Brecht, which, however, to a large extent duplicate material in the present volume. Also the following early reviews: 'Bert Brecht und seine neue Dramen', *Augsburger Neueste Nachrichten: Erzähler*, 8 March 1924; and 'Bert Brechts Lyrik', *Augsburger Neueste Nachrichten: Erzähler*, 7 March 1925.

Münsterer's literary works remain to a large extent unpublished. The following chronology gives some impression of what little was published during his lifetime:

1920 to 1928 – a few poems and short prose stories in the *Erzähler* and the *Münchner Landbote*.
1925 – 'Fünf Balladen'; and *Passional deutsch*, a cycle of 48 poems, both in special editions by the Ariadne-Verlag (Augsburg).
1926 to 1932 – various contributions to literary journals (*Orplid, Jüngste Dichtung*) and anthologies.
1932 to 1938 – short cycles of poems and a radio play broadcast by Bavarian Radio, and a couple of poems in newspapers.

1947 and 1950 – poems in the journals *Das Goldene Tor* and *Hoch-land*, and in newspapers.

A selection of Münsterer's poems has now appeared as: *Mancher Mann*, edited by Manfred Brauneck (Frankfurt, 1980). This volume also contains a brief essay about Münsterer with substantial quotations from the diary he kept in 1918/19.

Münsterer's important medical and anthropological publications span the years 1926 to 1967. Most of the former are concerned with venereal disease, vaccination and immunology. Most of the latter deal with talismans and Christian symbols, and also with popular medicine. The larger publications include: *Gonorrhoe – Probleme der Gegenwart* (Stuttgart, 1947); and *Grundlagen, Gültigkeit und Grenzen der volksmedizinischen Heilverfahren* (Darmstadt, 1967).

Münsterer's papers, including a great many literary manuscripts, are preserved in the Bayerisches Staatsarchiv, Munich.

Apart from scattered reviews, there is next to no secondary literature on Münsterer: Heinz Saueressig, 'Hanns Otto Münsterer: Dermatologe, Dichter und Volkskundeforscher' in: Saueressig, *Ärzte und Ärztliches: Essayistische Anregungen* (Biberach/Riss, 1989), and a brief entry in Hans J. Schütz, *'Ein deutscher Dichter bin ich einst gewesen': Vergessene und verkannte Autoren des 20. Jahrhunderts* (Munich, 1988).

Index of Names

This index is of names (including publishers and bookshops) in Münsterer's text and in the Preface, Editorial Introduction and 'Further Perspectives'. It does not include historical or mythological figures which feature only in works of literature.